*Our dear brother Paul also wrote you
with the wisdom that God gave him. . . .
His letters contain some things
that are hard to understand,
which ignorant and unstable people distort,
as they do the other Scriptures,
to their own destruction.
2 Peter 3:15-16*

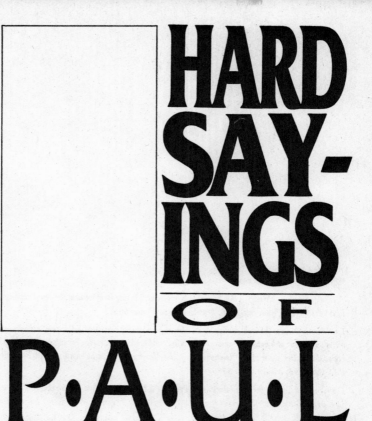

HARD SAY-INGS OF P·A·U·L

Manfred T. Brauch

INTERVARSITY PRESS
DOWNERS GROVE, ILLINOIS 60515

InterVarsity Press is the book-publishing division of InterVarsity Christian Fellowship, a student movement active on campus at hundreds of universities, colleges and schools of nursing. For information about local and regional activities, write Public Relations Dept., InterVarsity Christian Fellowship, 6400 Schroeder Rd., P.O. Box 7895, Madison, WI 53707-7895.

Distributed in Canada through InterVarsity Press, 860 Denison St., Unit 3, Markham, Ontario L3R 4H1, Canada.

All Scripture quotations, unless otherwise indicated, are from the Holy Bible, New International Version. Copyright © 1973, 1978, International Bible Society. Used by permission of Zondervan Bible Publishers.

Cover illustration: Dian Ameen-Newbern

ISBN 0-8308-1282-2

Printed in the United States of America ♾

Library of Congress Cataloging-in-Publication Data

Brauch, Manfred T.
Hard sayings of Paul/Manfred T. Brauch.
p.   cm.
Includes index.
ISBN 0-8308-1282-2
1. Bible.   N.T. Epistles of Paul—Criticism, interpretation, etc.
I. Title.
BS2650.2.B73   1989
227'.077—dc20   89-31814
                                                      CIP

17	16	15	14	13	12	11	10	9	8	7	6	5	4	3	2	1
99	98	97	96	95	94	93	92	91	90	89						

JustiCe vs. Grace ?

Preface

The theme for this book is contained in 2 Peter 3:15-16. Here we are told that the apostle Paul's writings, which speak everywhere of our Lord's gracious and patient work leading to our salvation, have in them "some things that are hard to understand, which ignorant and unstable people distort, as they do the other Scriptures, to their own destruction." Several basic insights emerge from this text which provide an important starting point for this book.

First, it is clear that Paul's writings, which come roughly from the period A.D. 50-65, have already begun to circulate rather widely. 2 Peter 3:16 refers to "all his letters." Since Paul wrote to churches and individuals across the Greco-Roman empire—from Rome in the West to Galatia in the East—some years must have elapsed for Paul's letters to have become known, distributed and read throughout the churches. Perhaps several decades have elapsed since Paul penned his epistles.

Second, Paul's letters have already attained quite a measure of authority. Though it is doubtful that Paul's writings were at this time already seen on a par with sacred Scriptures (that is, our Old Testament, which was early Christianity's Bible), the reference to "the other Scriptures" certainly indicates that the writings of Christ's apostle to the Gentiles are seen as an extension of the authoritative Word of both the Lord who meets us in the

Old Testament and of Christ, the Lord of the church.

Third, Peter's reference to "hard sayings" in Paul's letters shows that, as early as sometime in the second half of the first century, Christians in the churches had a difficult time accepting or understanding or properly applying certain of Paul's sayings. Now if this was true within the first few decades subsequent to the writing of Paul's letters, how much more is that likely the case for us, who are removed from Paul's time not only by the passing of about two thousand years, but also by such important aspects of human experience as history and culture and language. If it was possible back then to misunderstand or even twist the meaning of certain of Paul's sayings, it is very likely that this possibility is even greater for us.

A leading continental scholar of the last century, Adolf von Harnack, once said that the only one who ever really understood Paul was the second-century heretic Marcion, but that even he misunderstood Paul. Harnack's point was that Marcion clearly grasped the radical nature of Paul's gospel—namely, that salvation comes by God's grace, not by obedience to the Law—but that Marcion's rejection of the Old Testament on the basis of Paul's gospel represented a misunderstanding of Paul.

Thus, from the very early years of Christians' use of Paul's letters, the possibility of either understanding or misunderstanding, of either proper or improper use, have been ever-present realities. For us twentieth-century Christians, this fact ought to give both humility and hope. There may be times when, after careful and thorough study of a text, we should in all humility acknowledge that we simply cannot grasp the meaning or know definitely what the writer intends the reader to grasp. But there is always also the hope that careful study—always under the guidance of the Spirit—will lead us to a hearing of the "hard sayings" in such a way that God's Word can do its work in our lives.

The selection of "hard sayings of Paul" treated in this book emerges from this writer's experience as a Christian, a student and a teacher. In personal study, in work with college and seminary students, and in countless discussions with Christians in churches and non-Christians in the academy, these texts have again and again emerged as "problem texts." Some thoroughly confuse readers or create unresolved tension between the meaning of one text and another. Others seem obscure or unclear. Still others lead to different misunderstandings. And a few appear to be so out of character with the overall meaning and intention of the gospel that they meet with opposition or outright rejection, even by some who are deeply committed to the authority of the Bible for Christian faith and life.

It is my hope that this book will make a positive contribution in the continuing effort to provide a clearer understanding of some of the "hard sayings" of the Epistle literature.

The reader is urged to have a Bible at hand for easy reference, so that frequent mention of related biblical passages and the entire contexts of the "hard sayings" can be followed up and seen clearly. In this way, the study of the following chapters will be most fruitful. The basic English translation used in this book is the New International Version. When other versions are employed, it is indicated in the text.

· INTRODUCTION ·

Understanding and Interpreting Biblical Texts

The reading and study of any writing, if it is to be faithful to the author's purpose, must take seriously at least three things: (1) the nature of the writing itself, (2) the purpose for which it was written and (3) the situation or context out of which it was written. Failure to observe these matters is more likely than not to lead to misunderstanding or misinterpretation.

In this chapter we shall discuss the matters of nature, purpose and situation, giving particular attention to principles of biblical interpretation which will assist in the study of the selected texts.

But before we begin we must also recognize that every interpreter of Scripture, including me, comes to the text with certain assumptions about the material to be studied. I want you to know before we begin what my assumptions are.

In approaching these hard sayings of Paul, I write self-consciously from within the evangelical tradition of theology, personal faith and commitment. I write from a perspective that cherishes this heritage's deep and central commitment to the Bible as the ultimate criterion for our understanding and application of God's self-revelation, which finds its ultimate expression in the Incarnation. The fundamental affirmation of evangelical faith with regard to the Bible is that we have in this word of God's gracious self-disclosure an authentic, reliable record of God's truth and purposes which, when responded to in faith, leads to restored relationships with God and our fellow human beings. Scripture—including our "hard sayings"—is our authoritative, infallible guide for faith and life.

Having stated this presupposition, which is at its core an affirmation of faith, I must immediately admit that such a commitment does not in and of itself determine the interpretation of any scriptural text. What it does do is set a tone and provide limits. It means that if you share that assumption with me, we approach the texts, recognizing that they are more than the result of human thought and theological reflection—that they emerge from the ministry and teaching of Christ's commissioned apostles, who were led and inspired by the Spirit of Christ in their ministry of writing.

This assumption about the Bible also means that we cannot simply bypass, ignore or reject texts which may be difficult to reconcile with other aspects of Scripture or whose meaning or instruction we find difficult to accept. Our starting point obligates us to take such sayings with utmost seriousness, seeking to understand what they mean, why they were written, and what implications for our faith and life they have.

Such an obligation brings us directly into the arena of biblical hermeneutics, or interpretation, where persons who are equally committed to the assumptions about the inspiration and authority of the Bible stated above often come to different conclusions. The extent of such differences can be greatly reduced when we come to the hermeneutical task with equal commitment to take seriously the three items mentioned above: the nature of the writings, the situations out of which they were written, and the purposes for which they were written. To these matters we shall now turn.

The Nature and Purpose of Scripture

When we are concerned with the nature and purpose of the biblical text, we are immediately confronted with the issue of its authority, with its character as the word of God. How are we to understand this authoritative character in light of the fact that the biblical record consists of the writings of a great variety of persons in different historical periods in response to a host of events and situations and experiences?

To answer this question we need to be faithful to the intention of Scripture and take with utmost seriousness the fact that God's final, ultimate form of self-disclosure is the Incarnation.

In 2 Timothy 3:15-17 Paul speaks clearly about the nature of Scripture and its purpose: "You have known the holy Scriptures, which are able to make you wise for salvation through faith in Christ Jesus. All Scripture is God-breathed and is useful for teaching, rebuking, correcting and training in righteousness, so that the man of God may be thoroughly equipped for every good work."

It is divine inspiration that gives to the Bible its authoritative character. And that inspiration, while clearly enunciated in 2 Timothy, is implicitly affirmed throughout the New and Old Testaments by the use of such formulas as "God says" or "the Holy Spirit says" (2 Cor 6:16; Acts 1:16). God and Scripture were so intimately linked that "what Scripture says" and "what God says" could be equated (Rom 9:17; Gal 3:8). Jesus' use of and attitude toward the Old Testament strongly confirms this sense of Scripture's divine origin and content (see, for example, Mt 5:17-18; Jn 10:35). It is also clear from the New Testament that the words of Jesus and the witness of Jesus' apostles share the same inspiration and authority of the Old Testament (see, for example, Jn 10:25; 12:49; 1 Cor 2:13; 1 Thess 2:13; Heb 3:7).

That the Bible claims inspiration is evident then. But what is its intention? What is God's purpose for it? To make us wise for salvation, says Paul, and for teaching, rebuking, correcting and training in righteousness (2 Tim 3:15-16).

The biblical writings were written "to teach us, so that through endurance and the encouragement of the Scriptures we might have hope" (Rom 15:4). This redemptive purpose of inspired Scripture is also the point of John 20:31: "These are written that you may believe that Jesus is the Christ, the Son of God, and that by believing you may have life in his name."

The Acts 8 story of Philip's encounter with the Ethiopian is also instructive here. The understanding and interpretation of the Isaiah passage have one purpose: "Philip began with that very passage of Scripture and told him the good news about Jesus" (v. 35). That is the "what for," the purpose. Jesus did not recommend the Bible as a book of divinely given facts about things in general (science, history, anthropology, cosmology). Rather, he pointed to the Old Testament and said: "These are they which bear witness to me" (Jn 5:39). If our study of Scripture is isolated from these explicit purposes, our attempts to understand the "hard sayings" may prove futile.

The fact that the writers of our biblical documents were inspired does not mean that they were stripped of their limitations in knowledge, memory or language as specific human beings in certain periods of history. The presence of this human reality in Scripture has been acknowledged throughout the church's history. From Origen through Augustine to the Reformers and beyond, the reality of God's accommodation in Scripture to human weakness and limitation has been affirmed. The condescension of a nurse or a schoolmaster to the limitation of children has been used as an analogy. God stooped down to us and spoke the language of the recipients so that we might hear and understand him.

And we must recognize that it is precisely some of these accommodations to human limitations which make some of Paul's and other biblical writers' words difficult for us to understand, even while we continue to recognize the full authority of their words. Just as Jesus was fully human and yet fully divine—subject to human limitations and yet without sin—so Scripture, while manifesting many of the limitations of its human character, is yet fully God's authoritative Word to us.

While the paradoxical mystery of this juxtaposition of both the human and the divine—in the Incarnation of the Living Word and in the Written Word—defies final explication, the Gospel of Luke provides us with a key toward understanding. Luke presents Jesus as "conceived by the Spirit" and endowed with the Spirit at his baptism; as the one who, "full of the Spirit," is "led by the Spirit" into the wilderness; as the one who inaugurates his ministry "in the power of the Spirit" (Luke 1—4). For Luke the presence and power of the Spirit mediate the divine reality of Jesus in and through the human limitations. It is the Spirit who makes the incarnate Jesus' human words and actions effective. In his words and actions, God speaks and acts. Such an understanding of the Incarnation, when applied to Scripture, underlines its full humanity (with all that this implies regarding the presence of limitation) and its full divinity (with all that this implies about its authority). The hearing and believing of the divine authority, in and through the fully human, is made possible by the Spirit.

Recognizing both (1) the purpose for which the writers were inspired and (2) the limiting human form and context within which their inspiration took place is frequently an important key in understanding Paul's "hard sayings."

The Context of Biblical Texts

Beyond this general understanding of the nature and purpose of the Bible, the specific situations of particular biblical documents have an important bearing on our interpretation and understanding. Though it is necessary to keep this fact in mind regarding each biblical book, the "situational nature" of the Epistles is especially noteworthy.

The Epistles are occasional documents, that is they were written for specific occasions in the life of Christian congregations or individuals. They respond to questions which have been communicated to the writer (1 and 2 Thess), deal with problems in the church (1 Cor), carry on a debate with a false understanding of the gospel (Gal), nurture hope in a time of persecution (1 Pet) and seek to provide guidance for a pastor in a situation where false teachings and speculative mythology are threatening the integrity of the gospel and the stability of Christian community (1 and 2 Tim).

In addition to these unique needs which called forth the writing of the Epistles, the historical and cultural contexts of the recipients must also be recognized as factors which bear on our interpretation. Thus, when Paul addresses himself to the place of women in the worship of the church in Corinth and calls for certain restrictions, it is important to ask "Why does he give those instructions?" and to recognize that the cultural-religious environment in Corinth may have made these restrictions necessary in that particular situation, whereas in other situations such restrictions were not called for. Or when we read in 1 Timothy 2:11-12 that women are to "learn in quietness" and that they are not permitted "to teach or to have authority over a man," it is of critical importance to recognize that one of the major problems in Timothy's pastoral context was the presence of heretical teachings and mystical speculations, most likely perpetuated by leading women in that particular congregation. For in other early church settings, women were clearly involved in leadership, as well as in teaching and preaching functions.

The consideration of context probably introduces the most difficult issue in the whole task of interpretation: How can we discern between that which is culturally or historically conditioned and that which is transcultural or transhistorical? When is an apostolic instruction an inspired, authoritative word for a particular context in an early church setting and applicable only to that situation, and when is an inspired, authoritative instruction an absolute norm for any and all situations and contexts from the early church to this present day?

The effort to discern between those things which are culturally and historically relative and those which are transcendent is in actuality engaged in by all Christians, in one way or another. At issue is only whether such discernment results from our likes and dislikes, our own cultural conditioning and prejudices, or whether it is the application of a clear principle that emerges from a proper understanding of the nature and purpose of Scripture.

Take, for example, the issue of head coverings. Most Christians have concluded that the "head covering" enjoined upon women during worship in the church in Corinth (1 Cor 11) is culturally relative, and its inspired authority is limited to that historical situation. Many of these same Christians have concluded, at the same time, that Paul's instruction to these women to be silent in worship (1 Cor 14) is not culturally relative and is an authoritative word for all Christian women in all contexts of worship, both then and now.

On what basis is this distinction made? Arbitrariness in this critical and necessary area of biblical interpretation can to some extent be avoided when we recognize that there are different types of texts, and that these differences provide us with clues to discerning that which is relative to the situation and that which is authoritative for all time.

In an article in *Essays on New Testament Christianity*, S. Scott Bartchy gathers texts which deal directly or indirectly with the place and role of women in the ministry of Jesus and the early church into three broad categories: (1) normative (or instructive) texts, (2) descriptive texts and (3) problematic (or corrective) texts. These categories are extremely helpful for purposes of our discussion.

Instructive texts are those which declare the way things ought to be among the followers of Christ. They declare the vision or intention of the gospel without reference to particular problem situations. As such they transcend the contexts in which they are uttered and are normative for both individual and corporate Christian existence. The citation of Joel 2:28-32 in Peter's Pentecost speech (Acts 2:17-21), stating that the Spirit of God was given to both men and women for proclaiming the good news, is such a text.

Descriptive texts describe practices or actions in the early churches without any commentary. The sense conveyed in such texts is that what is described is perfectly acceptable or normal. The writer does not question the practice but rather seems to assume it as appropriate. Thus Luke, in Acts 18:24-26, tells us that both Priscilla and Aquila instructed the learned Apollos in the Christian faith, and in Acts 21:9 mentions that the evangelist Philip had four daughters who were engaged in the prophetic ministry of the church. Women's participation in ministry seems not to have been unusual.

Corrective texts are those which clearly deal with special situations or problems or misunderstandings in the Christian communities which are addressed. Here it is particularly important to understand as much as possible the situation which made the corrective, authoritative, apostolic word necessary for that situation. The problem of heretical teaching, addressed in 1 Timothy, is such a situation. Paul's instruction about the silence of women must be seen in this light. What we must guard against is the temptation to universalize instructions whose primary or exclusive focus was on the situation addressed.

An important dimension of this threefold classification for the interpretation and understanding of a good number of our "hard sayings" is the matter of their interrelationships. If a corrective text's admonition reflects the vision of the gospel articulated in instructive texts and is further confirmed by descriptive texts, then the particular teaching would undoubtedly be authoritative for the whole church in all times. On the other hand, if an apostolic word addressed to a particular setting does not conform to the way things ought to be (as revealed in instructive texts) and the way things normally are (as revealed in descriptive texts), then the inspired, authoritative word may very well be intended to deal exclusively with a specific problem and thus be limited to that and similar problems.

The foregoing reflections on the nature, purpose and context of biblical texts provide the parameters within which we will explore the "hard sayings of Paul." For readers interested in further and more comprehensive study of the issues in biblical interpretation, I highly recommend the book *How to Read the Bible for All Its Worth* (Zondervan, 1982) by Gordon D. Fee and Douglas Stuart.

• CHAPTER 1 •

Is God Wrathful?

*The wrath of God is being revealed
from heaven against all the godlessness
and wickedness of men who
suppress the truth.*
ROMANS 1:18

God's wrath is difficult both to understand and to believe. For some, the idea of a wrathful God has been a roadblock to faith. For others, who have experienced the transforming grace and love of God in their lives, the idea of God's wrath has seemed to contradict their experience of God. Can we believe that the God whose unconditional love is revealed "in that, while we were yet sinners, Christ died for us" (Rom 5:8) is at the same time a God of wrath?

Before we tackle the main issues here, we need to discuss the biblical use of anthropomorphisms—the use of analogies from human experience to describe God. The Bible speaks about God's nature, work and purposes in terms analogous to what we know and experience as human beings. This is by necessity. God's absolute nature is not open to finite creatures. We can only approximate what God is like by comparing him to us. Indeed, the Incarnation, God's coming into our midst in the Word become flesh (Jn 1:14), gives legitimacy and authority to anthropomorphic speech about God.

In traditional theological language, this necessary and legitimate use of anthropomorphisms has been recognized, but it also has its limitations. Thus, while knowledge and power are aspects of human experience, God is said to possess these in an absolute, infinite sense: he is *omniscient* (all-knowing) and *omnipotent* (all-powerful). Generally, those aspects of human nature and experience which we have identified as the highest and the best have been ascribed to God. We see God as the one who is or possesses truth, grace, beauty, love, righteousness, faithfulness in their most complete or absolute forms. But a corollary of this way of speaking about God is the resistance to ascribe to God human attributes or feelings which we perceive as negative: hate, anger, a vindictive spirit, ugliness, and so forth. Wrath is clearly one of these.

There is some biblical warrant for this resistance. For example, in Hosea 11, the reason for God's refusal to give up on Israel—though she clearly deserved destruction on the basis of human standards of justice—is the fact that "I am God and not man" (Hos 11:9). However, the major reason for our difficulty in accepting such negative human attributes for God is an idealistic, romantic notion of God, born from philosophical speculation. The Bible does not have such a notion of God, for it takes both God and the world more seriously than abstract philosophical speculation.

The Lord of the Bible enters into relationship with his creation in Jesus of Nazareth, in whom "all the fullness of God was

pleased to dwell" (Col 1:19). It is this Jesus who is, at the same
time, "in all respects like us" (Heb 2:17). The Bible also takes the
relationship between Creator and creation with utmost seriousness. Because the creation is God's, it is responsible to God.
Within such a relationship of accountability, romantic, idealistic,
sentimental concepts of God are out of place. Against this larger
background the concept of God's wrath must be understood.

It is instructive that Paul speaks of the revelation of God's
wrath within the context of a theology of creation. The biblical
story of creation and alienation contained in the opening chapters of Genesis clearly forms the backdrop of Romans 1:18-23.
Especially verses 21-22 are a poignant reminder of the refusal of
humankind (Adam) to live as creature in relationship with God
and instead to grasp for likeness with God (see Gen 3:1-7).

In the Genesis narrative, the temptation is to deny our creatureliness, our limitations, our dependence on the Creator in
order to become "like God" (Gen 3:5). The result of that denial
is that we become debased, less than authentically human. According to the narrative of Genesis 3—11, the denial of dependence on and accountability to God results in a wide variety of
distortions within various spheres of human community. Paul,
in Romans 1:25, sums up this situation with these words:
"They exchanged the truth of God for a lie, and worshiped and
served created things rather than the Creator." It is within this
assessment of God's purposes for creation and its refusal to be
accountable within those purposes that the idea of God's wrath
needs to be heard.

Paul speaks of the wrath of God in two ways. Mostly, the
expression refers to a future event in which God's judgment is
executed on the world's sinfulness (Rom 2:5,8; 5:9; Eph 5:6, 1
Thess 1:10; 5:9). In these contexts, God's wrath (or its synonym,
God's judgment) is clearly perceived as an activity of God, his
decided action against sin. It is important to note here that wrath

is God's personal response to sin, though unlike that of the various divinities of Greco-Roman religions and myths, God's wrath is never capricious, vindictive or malicious.

In our text, Paul does not say that God's wrath *will be* revealed at the last day (that is, judgment day) but rather, "God's wrath is being revealed from heaven now." It is not only the divine response to the creation's unfaithfulness in the future judgment; it is already a present reality. This sense of a present manifestation of God's wrath is confirmed in several other passages from Paul (Rom 3:5; 4:15; 9:22; 1 Thess 2:16), as well as in other New Testament writings (see Jn 3:36).

As the passage which follows 1:18 shows, the present manifestation of God's wrath is *indirect* rather than *direct;* it is an expression of God's permissive will, not God's active will. God is not depicted here as doing something in response to human sin. In some sense, God's wrath is built into the very structure of created reality. In rejecting God's structure and establishing our own, in violating God's intention for the creation and substituting our own intentions, we cause our own disintegration.

The human condition, which Paul describes in 1:18-32, is not something caused by God. The phrase, "revealed from heaven" (where "heaven" is a typical Jewish substitute word for "God"), does not depict some kind of divine intervention, but rather the *inevitability of human debasement* which results when God's will, built into the created order, is violated. Since the created order has its origin in God, Paul can say that the wrath of God is now (constantly) being revealed "from heaven." It is revealed in the fact that the rejection of God's truth (1:18-20), that is, the truth about God's nature and will, leads to futile thinking (1:21-22), idolatry (1:23), perversion of God-intended sexuality (1:24-27) and relational-moral brokenness (1:28-32).

The expression "God gave them over" (or "handed them over"), which appears three times in our passage (1:24, 26, 28), supports the idea that the sinful perversion of human existence, though resulting from human decisions, is to be understood ultimately as God's punishment which we, in freedom, bring upon ourselves.

In light of these reflections on our text, the common notion that God punishes or blesses in direct proportion to our sinful or good deeds, cannot be maintained. God's relationship with us is not on a reciprocal basis. God's radical, unconditional love has been demonstrated in that, while we were sinners, Christ died for us. God loves us with an everlasting love. But the rejection of that love separates us from its life-giving power. The result is disintegration and death. Against such a perverted creation, God's wrath is revealed.

• CHAPTER 2 •

One Man's Sin Means My Death?

*Sin entered the world
through one man,
and death through sin.*
ROMANS 5:12

Why should the sin of the first human being become the downfall
of the entire race? Why should all subsequent human beings
stand under God's judgment against a basic sinfulness for which
none of us is ultimately responsible? How, in the face of such
claims, are we to believe that God is just?

These and other problems arise out of this text that has provided the basis for commonly held doctrines about the nature of
the human predicament. But many such questions are the result
of improper interpretations or misunderstandings of the text.

The word *sin* (and its synonym, *trespass*) is the key word in
Romans 5:12, as well as in Paul's description of the human con-

dition in the first three chapters of this epistle. What does Paul mean by that term? What is his understanding of the origin of the human situation which he describes with this term?

Paul's understanding of human sinfulness is expressed in two phrases: (1) "they did not think it worthwhile to retain the knowledge of God" (Rom 1:28) and (2) "you rely on the law and brag about your relationship to God" (2:17). Sin is seen as refusal to accept our creatureliness, to acknowledge our dependence on our Maker, to recognize our limitations. "We are sinners" does not mean, primarily, that we have moral problems, but that in the deepest and final sense we are severed from relationship with God because of refusal or bragging.

Sin is not a *thing*. Nor is sin a *genetic defect*. The idea that sin is passed on genetically, and thereby becomes the property of each individual through heredity, ultimately led to a low view of sex. Sex is seen as the prime locus of human sinfulness—to be tolerated for the purpose of procreation, but not as a part of God's economy for human wholeness and fulfillment.

Nor is sin a *perverted inner nature*. The problem with this understanding of sin is that it divides the individual into a number of separate boxes. It arises from the idea that the Fall resulted in the perversion of one essential part of our selves. A number of candidates have been proposed. For some, the perverted part is the will. For others, it is the emotions or passions. For still others, it is reason. The pervasive mood of anti-intellectualism in some circles of Christians is traceable to such an understanding. Since the mind was affected by the Fall, our reasoning capacity is perverted and depraved and the quest of the mind cannot be trusted.

But such a view does not do justice to all the biblical data. As total persons we are fallen and stand under the judgment of God. Both our heads *and* hearts stand under the signature of death. Both are dust.

From the biblical point of view, the term *sin* designates a par-

ticular kind of relationship between the creature and the Creator. And a relationship cannot be inherited; it can only be established or destroyed, affirmed or denied. Sin is thus a *relational
reality.*

We are sinners insofar as we are unrelated to God. The questions raised by that statement are: *Why* are we that? *Why* is that
our condition? *Why* do we find ourselves in such a dilemma?
Paul's answer to such questions is found in Romans 5:12-13.

Our text has traditionally been seen as the biblical foundation
for the Christian doctrine of original sin: "We all stand under the
Fall of first man; that is why we are in the mess we are in!" But
this view is inadequate. For Paul does not say that we sin *because*
Adam sinned. He does not say that we die *because* Adam sinned.
What he does say is this: Sin (alienation from God) entered the
stage of history in the first man's rebellion ("sin entered the
world through one man"). The result of that separation is disintegration and death. But the universal penetration of that condition is due to the fact that all persons have sinned; all persons
have become revolutionaries against God ("because all sinned").

There is a two-sided perspective here in Paul which must be
taken seriously if we wish to understand him adequately. On the
one side of this dual perspective is the Hebrew idea of *human
solidarity,* the recognition that each individual shares in a common
humanity. On the other side is the recognition of *individual responsibility.* By virtue of the former, we are in bondage; by virtue of
the latter, we become responsible for participation in that bondage. Let us look at that duality in more detail.

Human solidarity. Paul was heir to a tradition concerning the
human condition which was deeply rooted in Jewish beliefs. That
tradition recognized the intimate interdependence of individuals
and the effect that such solidarity could have, both positively and
negatively. The Old Testament concept that the sins of parents
would have their effect down through several generations re-

flects the Hebrew idea of corporate solidarity. The immediate background for Paul's statements concerning the relation between first man and the rest of humankind (5:12-21) can be clearly seen in a Jewish work of the first century A.D.

> [Adam] transgressed. . . . Thou didst appoint death for him and for his descendants. . . .
> For the first Adam, burdened with an evil heart, transgressed and was overcome, as were also all who were descended from him. Thus the disease became permanent.
> (2 Esdras 3:7, 21-22)

> O Adam, what have you done? For though it was you who sinned, the fall was not yours alone, but ours also who are your descendants. (2 Esdras 7:118)

Paul clearly reflects this Jewish understanding in 5:12-13. Adam, the typical, representative first human being yields to the temptation to determine his own existence and his own destiny (that is, he sins). The result of that self-determination is death. Death is the condition of separateness, since the creature apart from the Creator does not have life. Physical death is clearly a part of this picture in the Hebrew-Pauline understanding. Separation from the source of life results in decay and disintegration.

But both for the Old Testament and for Paul, death is also an existential reality, a real condition of life. Thus Ezekiel receives a vision of "dry bones" that are representative of the failure of Israel to be and remain God's people (Ezek 37). Hosea can speak of the resurrection of Israel from the grave of its national downfall (Hos 6:2). And Paul can speak of Christians as those "who have been brought from death to life" (Rom 6:13). The uniform affirmation of this biblical tradition is that there exists a mysterious relationship between human self-determination and death and between the first man's self-determination and our own death. We belong to one another, and the condition of one has inevitable consequences for others.

Sociological and psychological studies have confirmed that scriptural understanding of human solidarity. We have been shown how heredity, upbringing and environment play major roles in the formation of our personalities. I am, to a large degree, the product of my world. What I am in the present is a continuation of all that I have assumed—consciously and unconsciously—from my past. Thus the child raised in an environment with violent models is more likely to be involved in violent behavior than those not raised with such models. The child of psychologically disturbed parents is more likely to become neurotic than the child of mentally healthy parents. The child who grows up in a broken home is less likely to become a whole, healthy person than one raised in a home with genuine love and caring from both parents in a consistent and stable relationship.

All of us are born into a human community that is overshadowed by the cumulative weight of human sinfulness, oppressive structures, prejudices, injustices. We are, all of us, more or less affected by the shadows which these clouds cast over our motives and orientations, our attitudes and priorities.

Individual Responsibility. In Romans 5:12-21, Paul not only reflects Jewish religious thought that we share a common humanity and that we are affected by that interdependence, he also reflects the Jewish belief that as individuals we are responsible and held accountable for the way we relate to that common humanity.

Already at the time of Ezekiel, a protest was raised against the ancient Hebrew idea that the sins of parents will be visited upon the children and that the children will be held accountable for their parent's transgressions. In Ezekiel 18, the prophet speaks the decisive word of God for individual responsibility:

Yet you ask, "Why does the son not share the guilt of his father?" Since the son has done what is just and right, . . . he will surely live. The soul who sins is the one who will die. The son will not share the guilt of the father. (Ezek 18:19-20)

This concept of individual responsibility made itself increasingly felt and is clearly enunciated in Jewish writings close to the time of Paul. In the Wisdom of Solomon, which dates from the first century B.C., the author discusses the presence of evil in the world in clear allusion to Genesis 2:

Do not invite death by the error of your life,
    nor bring on destruction by the works of your hands;
because God did not make death. . . .
But ungodly men by their words and deeds summoned death.
    (1:12-13, 16 RSV)

The parallel between this understanding of individual responsibility and Paul's statement in Romans 5:12 is unmistakable. The same idea is voiced in a Jewish book of the first century A.D., the Apocalypse of Baruch:

Adam is therefore not the cause, save only of his own soul,
But each of us has been the Adam of his own soul.
    (2 Baruch 54:19)

What Paul affirms in 5:12 together with his Jewish background is that each person continues the rebellion and self-determination of Adam in his or her own life. It is in that sense that each of us becomes a part of that fateful history which stands under the signature of death. Each individual participates in the Adamic humanity and becomes accountable for that participation. Death marches across the pages of human history because humans in their own individuality have sinned. They do what Adam did. And the attempt to determine our own existence, however that may work itself out in everyday living, leads to separation from God.

Paul, in our text, affirms both parts of Jewish teaching about the origin and nature of sin: we stand in mysterious solidarity with *Adam* (Eve and Adam) in sin; we are also individually responsible. There is a sense in which we are determined; there is another sense in which we are absolutely free. But since we are both, neither the one nor the other is the final word.

This Pauline understanding of sin as dynamic, relational reality leads directly to *what is* his final word; namely, that this paradoxical reality of our bondage to, and freedom from, sin is overcome in *a new relationship*—one with Jesus Christ. Through that relationship, we are reconciled to God and in Christ we become members of *a new humanity*.

· C H A P T E R 3 ·

Increasing
Sin

*The law was added so that
the trespass might increase.*
ROMANS 5:20

On first reading, Romans 5:20 seems to suggest that the purpose of
the law of God, given to Moses for the people of Israel, was to
increase human sinfulness. But is it possible that the God revealed in our Lord Jesus Christ deliberately acted in such a way
that sin increased? Doesn't the revelation of God, from beginning to end of redemptive history as recorded in the Bible, tell
about a God who seeks to bring his lost and fallen creation back
into restored relationship with himself?

In order to hear Paul accurately, the context of this passage
needs to be considered, as well as several other statements about
the purpose of the law.

In Romans 5:12-21 Paul presents the contrast between the devastating consequences of human sinfulness and the magnificence of God's gift of salvation in Jesus Christ. Sin entered the human sphere through Adam's decision to reject God's purposes and gained universal dominance through continuing human disobedience (5:12). Having established this, Paul recognizes immediately that though sin has been here from the start, the law was given much later (5:13). The point is this: Even though individuals could not be held accountable for a standard which did not yet exist, they are part of a corporate humanity alienated from God and his good purposes (5:13-14).

Within this understanding of the corporate solidarity of human sin and individual responsibility, verse 20 must be understood. "The law was added so that the trespass might increase" cannot mean that God intended to increase sin. Paul has already shown both sin and its consequence, death, to be a universal reality. It cannot increase beyond this. What sin can be greater than that which separates the whole creation from its Creator?

Thus, the meaning of the passage must be that the law was given to "increase the awareness, the consciousness of sin." Its destructive, devastating nature is revealed for what it really is when the good intentions of God, expressed in the law, are violated.

Throughout the Old Testament, and in rabbinic interpretations of those narratives which tell of the giving of the law to Israel, it is clear that the law was actually understood as a gift from God. Paul shared this view (see Rom 7:10). But in disobeying the law humankind revealed the magnitude of its brokenness.

This understanding of verse 20 is confirmed in several similar statements made by Paul elsewhere. In Romans 3:20, he says that "through the law we become conscious of sin." In 7:7-8 he clearly exonerates the law. It is not the law which leads to sin.

Rather, it simply shows what sin looks like and how it expresses itself: "I would not have known what sin was except through the law." Finally, in Galatians 3:19, Paul asks the question, "What, then, was the purpose of the law?" and then supplies the answer, "It was added because of transgressions."

When all of these insights are taken together, it becomes clear that "increasing sin" does not refer to the accumulation of sins nor to greater sins (as opposed to lesser sins). Rather, in light of both the law and God's grace in Christ (5:20-21), human sin is exposed and revealed to our consciousness in all its magnitude.

• C H A P T E R 4 •

Dead
to
Sin

We died to sin;
how can we live in it
any longer? . . . Anyone who has
died has been freed from sin.
ROMANS 6:2, 7

The basic dilemma expressed in this question and answer is the relationship between our new life in Christ—a life freed from sin—
and our actual day-to-day living, where sin in fact is all too often
present. In order to grasp Paul in this matter, we must first
attempt to understand his language about the nature of the believer's relationship to Christ.

The theme of Romans 6 is the contrast between an existence
characterized by death and one characterized by life. The former
is in view when Christians permit their new life in Christ to be
infiltrated by the forces of sin, by their former life "in Adam."
The latter is in view when Christians increasingly yield to the

claims that Christ has upon them.

The way of belonging to the new humanity, established in Christ, is expressed by Paul in language which is very mystical. He speaks of believers as those who have been "crucified" and "buried" with Christ; as having "died" and been "raised" with him. These phrases suggest an intense union between the believer and Christ that we, who have been thoroughly conditioned by rationalistic, scientific and technological thinking, have difficulty grasping. Perhaps Eastern mysticism and various cults with their meditation and inwardness prove so attractive because our civilized, acculturated form of Christianity fails to provide people with a sense of the mysterious, a sense of the "otherness" of the divine.

Paul's idea of *being in Christ,* or *being united with Christ,* has often been referred to as "Pauline mysticism," where "mysticism" designates a particularly intense relationship between the human and the divine. What was Paul's understanding of the nature of the mystical relationship between the believer and the Lord?

In Romans 6:1-10, Paul tells us that entrance into the new humanity is by means of an intense union with Christ which he presents by use of baptismal imagery of immersion: going into the waters of baptism and emerging from them symbolizes one's dying and rising with Christ. Further, the way of belonging to the new humanity is expressed in two ways:

1. By way of negation: we are dead to sin (6:2), no longer enslaved by sin (6:6), freed from sin (6:7) because the old self was crucified (6:6).

2. By way of affirmation: there is newness of life (6:4), union with Christ (6:5) and life with him (6:8) because a new self emerged in our being raised with him (6:4).

Now in these images what is extremely interesting, as well as puzzling, is that Paul presents them as statements of both *fact* and *possibility*. In the Greek language the indicative mood is employed to make factual assertions. In the context of our passage, Paul uses the indicative mood to assert without equivocation the *fact* that believers are dead to sin, freed from sin, crucified with Christ and so forth. Side by side with these assertions, Paul uses the subjunctive mood, which in Greek is used to express possibility, to express the *hope* that believers, as a result of being crucified and risen with Christ, might no longer be enslaved by sin (6:6) and might walk in newness of life (6:4).

What we have here is the presence of a real tension between the affirmation that we died to sin and are therefore free from its bondage, and the assertion that such freedom is always and only present as a possibility which must be actualized.

How are we to understand this paradoxical juxtaposition of both fact and possibility? Perhaps another look at the baptismal imagery can help us, since Paul clearly associates baptism with the death and resurrection of Christ and with our dying to sin and rising to newness of life.

Baptism has been understood in the various Christian traditions as either sacramental, or mystical-spiritual, or symbolic. In the first, the event is seen as actually mediating the saving qualities of the death and resurrection of Christ. In the second, the event is understood to signal the real presence of the crucified and risen Christ and an inner, spiritual union between Christ and the baptized person. In the third, the event is seen as an external symbol of movement from death to life, resulting from personal decision, commitment and faith.

This is not the place to argue the merits or demerits of these major positions and their variations. All of them have been supported with weighty theological arguments. But it may be possible to combine the deepest truths expressed in these various understandings in a way which also sheds new light on the paradox between fact and possibility in the life of the believer.

In Romans, Paul teaches that the work of God, accomplished in Christ and received by faith, leads to our justification or restored relationship with God. Since the sign of that transaction or restoration is baptism, it may be possible to view baptism in *relational terms*. In baptism we affirm that the life of the one who is baptized is henceforth to be determined by the fact that Christ died and was raised, that *in relationship with him* as justified persons, we are delivered from the dominion of sin and freed for life.

The dynamic of such a relational understanding allows us to deal with the paradoxical nature of new life in Christ, expressed so strongly in the indicative "He who has died is freed from sin" (6:7) and the imperative "Let not sin therefore reign . . ." (6:12).

New life, says Paul, has become both a reality and a possibility. How do we know that? Paul's answer is given in 6:9-10. Christ is alive; death no longer has dominion over him. Therefore, according to 6:11, we affirm that in relationship with him we are dead to sin and alive to God. The following passage (6:12-23) then speaks about the practical outworking of this life-giving relationship.

Let us illustrate this point from ordinary human experience. The relationship between a man and a woman in the covenant of marriage exists on two levels. There is that reality which exists on the basis of their mutual commitment in love and interdependence. On the second level is the practical incarnation of that reality, that commitment in concrete acts in everyday living.

Now it is clear that the relational reality, existing on the level of commitment, does not translate automatically or inevitably into the incarnational reality of everyday life. As C. S. Lewis put it, "[There is the possibility] of disappointment . . . on the threshold of every human endeavor. . . . It occurs when lovers get married and begin the real task of learning to live together. . . . [There is] the transition from dreaming aspiration to laborious doing."

In every relationship, there must constantly be movement from *affirmation* to *incarnation,* or else it is in difficulty. There are all sorts of threats and temptations which must be rejected again and again. To be married means that our lives are governed by the continual affirmation and incarnation of the commitments in that covenant. To be "in Christ," to be united with him in death and resurrection, means that our lives are determined by the continual affirmation and incarnation of the commitments in that relationship. In our relationship with Christ we are free from the *bondage to sin;* yet it is possible even for the Christian to "let sin reign" (6:12).

What does our life look like when affirmation is not translated into incarnation? When our relationship with Christ does not impinge on our everyday living, then other relationships will certainly fill this vacuum. If it is not the Lord Christ whose mind is being brought to bear upon our human relationships, then other lords will most certainly bring their minds to bear upon them.

Parents are models for their children, whether they like it or not. Our children sense very quickly who we are and what the lords and gods are at whose altars we serve. So the questions for me as a father are these: Do my children sense, as they are maturing, that my life is ruled by a higher kind of authority than tomorrow's paycheck, the expectations of my neighbors, the priority of things over persons? Do they sense, as they observe my relations with their mother, that we share a real love, that we are truly there for one another, that we keep pace, in that relationship, with a "different drummer"? To the extent that they sense these things, my life is an incarnation of my relationship with Christ. To the extent that they do not observe these, my life is an incarnation of other relationships.

Christian life is lived between the *indicative* ("you are raised
with Christ") and the *imperative* ("let not sin reign in your mortal
body"). Only by the empowering presence of God's Spirit can the
imperative find realization in our living.

· CHAPTER 5 ·

A Slave
to
Sin

We know that the law is spiritual;
but I am unspiritual, sold as a slave
to sin. . . . For what I do is not the good
I want to do; no, the evil I do not
want to do—this I keep on doing.
ROMANS 7:14, 19

On plain reading, what we have in this text is the candid confession of a basic split within the person, of an inner division which leads to utter weakness. Paul's final word about this condition is caught up in 7:24, "Wretched man that I am! Who will deliver me from this body of death?"

If this passage and the verses that surround it in chapter 7 are a description of what Christian life is all about, then it stands in stark contrast to the joy and freedom and newness with which Paul describes the Christian's life in chapters 5, 6 and 8. Indeed, it would seem that the "good news" of the gospel, expressed with such exuberance in 5:1 and 5:11, has become the "bad news." For how can Paul say, in 6:6, that "our old self was crucified with him" so that "we might no longer be enslaved to sin," and then go on to say, in 7:25, that "with my flesh I serve the law of sin"?

Yet, despite these difficulties, the most common understanding of this text is that Paul is here speaking about an internal tension between the Christian's higher and lower selves. Some have even used this text as a biblical warrant for unchristian behavior, as a cop-out from Christian responsibility.

As so often, it is important that both the immediate and wider context of this text be grasped if we are properly to understand Paul's meaning. When we do that, it becomes difficult to maintain the usual understanding of the text.

Paul's discussion of justification on the basis of God's work in Christ (Rom 1—6) shows that the whole person is reconciled to God—body, soul and spirit. Justification does not create a new moral or spiritual core within us which then has to fight it out with the rest of our being, our "baser instincts," our "flesh" with its passions and desires.

That idea rests on both a misunderstanding of certain words which Paul uses and an inadequate hearing of Paul's intention, revealed in the structure of the argument in chapter 7.

The troublesome word in 7:5-25 is the word *flesh*, used several times in association with the dominion of sin and death (verses 5, 18, 25). It is the contrast between "flesh" and the "I" with its higher aspirations which is largely responsible for the view that Romans 7 talks about a divided self in which constant warfare is raging.

When Paul speaks about "being in the flesh" throughout his writings, he is not talking about our physical nature as such, about physical passions and desires, but about a way of life, an orientation of life, a life lived apart from God's purposes for us. The Ephesians are told that they have been made alive, released from "the passions of the flesh." The passage then goes on to define "passions of the flesh" as "desires of body and mind" (Eph 2:1-3). This then defines the religious use of the term *flesh*, which for Paul included what in Greek thought was understood as the highest part of the human being, the mind.

A similar use of *flesh* is found in Romans 8. In drawing a contrast between two ways of life, Paul speaks of one way as "living according to the flesh," "setting the mind on the flesh," "being in the flesh" (8:5-8). Then he says: "But you are not in the flesh." Obviously, *flesh* is used here not with any physical, biological connotations. Rather, the religious use of the word *flesh* makes it possible for Paul to say that there *was* a time when "we were living in the flesh" (7:5) with the full recognition that Christians *continue* to be physical creatures.

When Paul, therefore, contrasts a "fleshly" with a "spiritual" way of living, he is not speaking about two distinct parts of the total self, but about two possible life-orientations of that total self. In the contrast between the "I" and "my flesh" (7:18), the "I" represents the total self insofar as it affirms the good, the will of God as expressed in the Law; "my flesh" represents the total self insofar as it is powerless, dominated by sin, unrelated to God.

Beside these considerations of Paul's terminology, the structure of the argument supports the thesis that Romans 7:7-25 is not a description of "life in Christ." In 7:5 and 7:6, Paul contrasts the former life ("while we were living in the flesh") with the new life ("but now"). These verses serve as topical sentences for what follows: verses 7-25 provide the interpretation of 7:5, while chapter 8 interprets 7:6. The former describes existence unto death; the latter, existence unto life.

Let us briefly trace the argument in 7:7-25. Since the law exposes our sinfulness (7:5), is the law therefore sin (7:7)? By no means! For the law is holy and spiritual, just and good (7:7-14). The reason we are in bondage to sin is because we are "fleshly" (7:14—remember our discussion above about this term). Now

Paul goes on in verses 15-24 to explain what it means to be "fleshly, sold under sin." It means that we fail to accomplish God's will, even though we acknowledge the goodness of God's law, even though we intend to live our lives accordingly (vv. 15-16). The self is so thoroughly in bondage to sin that one can indeed speak of a life in which the "I," which acknowledges God's law, is not in control (vv. 17-23). The result of such bondage is "wretchedness" (v. 24). But now there is a new way: Through Jesus Christ our Lord, we are freed from this desperate condition in which, though we serve the law of God with our mind, our concrete, actual living is "fleshly," dominated by sin (v. 25). In the next verse (8:1), Paul begins the description of this new life in Christ, this new life of the Spirit.

What Paul has given us in these verses of chapter 7 is a description of the ultimate futility of life lived in external conformity to law, even though that law is God's law. Clearly, Paul's encounter with Christ on the Damascus Road and beyond caused him to see his former life "under the law" as bondage from this new vantage point. Now, he wants his readers in Rome, as well as us, to understand that legalistic religion leads to death. Only the grace of God revealed and enacted in Jesus sets us free from bondage to sin to experience the "glorious liberty of the children of God" (8:21).

· C H A P T E R 6 ·

All Things for Good

And we know that in all things
God works for the good
of those who love him,
who have been called according
to his purpose.
ROMANS 8:28

The apparent discrepancy between its profound affirmation of faith
and our human experience makes Romans 8:28 one of the difficult sayings of Paul. For how can we see the hand of God at
work in the killing of a young child by a drunken driver? Where
are God's loving purposes revealed in the agony of a cancer vic-
tim's last weeks? What measure of good can be discerned in the
massacre of a Christian congregation by guerrillas? All these
kinds of experiences and events seem to contradict Paul's affirmation. It is therefore imperative that we understand what it is
that Paul is saying and how, in light of his own experience, he
was able to say it.

Apart from anything else which might be said about this text, it is clear within the context of chapter 8 that it expresses Paul's deep faith and trust in the loving purposes of God. We must remember that this affirmation is not the result of abstract rationalization or theologizing. It is, furthermore, not a word which emerges from the lips of one whose life coasted along in serenity, uninterrupted by the stresses and strains, the pains and perplexities, the turmoil and tragedies which most human beings experience to one degree or another.

No, this word of confidence and hope is written by one who, according to his own testimony in an earlier correspondence, was "unbearably crushed" and "despaired of life itself" (2 Cor 1:8); he was "afflicted in every way" and "perplexed," "persecuted" and "struck down" (2 Cor 4:8-9); he experienced "beatings," "imprisonments," "hardships" and "hunger" (2 Cor 6:4-5). It seems clear from the life and experience of Paul that we have in Romans 8:28 no "armchair theory," but a profound affirmation of faith that emerges out of experience which, on the surface at least, would not seem to support that affirmation.

What then is the "good" toward which God works? I believe we can only discover that when we take the whole context of the passage seriously. In verses 1-18 of chapter 8, Paul shows that Christians are people who are "in Christ" (8:1), whose existence is determined and empowered by the Spirit of Christ who dwells within (8:9-11). On the basis of this reality, we are "children of God" and "heirs with Christ" (8:16-17). We are therefore no longer in bondage to "the law of sin and death" (8:2).

But to be free from the enslaving realities of sin and death does not mean that we can live our lives unaffected by the continuing presence of sin and death in this world. And it is precisely this dual reality of "freedom from" as well as "continuing experience of" which Paul deals with in the second part of chapter 8.

Paul concludes his description of "life in Christ" or "life in the

Spirit" by affirming in verse 17 that this new life is lived in the tension between present suffering and final glorification. That is to say, freedom from bondage to sin and death does not mean the absence of either the reality of sin and death or the experience of this reality in the present.

The present reality of "peace with God" and "justification" (5:1) is but the first installment of God's gracious, redemptive action in Christ. There is much more yet to come. The "not-yet" dimension is already anticipated in Romans 5: beyond the present experience of being at "peace with God," there is the "hope of sharing the glory of God" (5:2) and the expectation of being "saved by his life" in the final judgment (5:9-10). This "not-yet" aspect of God's redemptive purpose is taken up again in our chapter 8. In verse 11 Paul points to the future resurrection of our "mortal bodies," which in verse 17 he refers to as our "glorification." Then in verse 18 he goes on to show "the sufferings of this present time" need to be placed in proper perspective in light of "the glory that is to be revealed."

In verses 18-25 our experiences, which do not seem "good" at all, are placed in the context of the totality of God's creation, which "waits with eager longing" (v. 19) and which is presently "subjected to futility" (v. 20) and in "bondage to decay" (v. 21). It is a creation which "has been groaning in travail" (v. 22) just as we human beings "groan inwardly" (v. 22). And just as the total creation "will be set free from its bondage to decay and obtain the glorious liberty of the children of God" (v. 21), so we can anticipate "the redemption of our bodies" (v. 23).

The proper attitude for our living between the first installment of our redemption and its final culmination is hope and patience (vv. 24-25). Our present situation, says Paul, is a situation of "weakness" (v. 26). If it were not so, patience and hope would not be necessary. Yet it is precisely in the midst of our weakness that the Spirit of God is present and working (vv. 26-27).

Verse 28, and the paragraphs which follow, must be seen within the context of the redemptive purposes of God outlined above. In all things—in our suffering, groaning, hoping, waiting; in "tribulation, or distress, or persecution, or famine, or nakedness, or peril, or sword" (8:35)—in all things God is working "toward the good" (8:28). That "good" is the final and complete realization of God's love for creation, incarnated in Christ, from which nothing can separate us (8:39).

"In all these things," Paul is convinced, we can be "more than conquerors" (8:37). Not on the basis of our efforts, nor on the basis of blind faith, nor through a kind of stoic resignation, but rather "through him who loved us" (8:37) and called us "according to his purpose" (8:28). That good and loving purpose finds its completion when the whole creation, including our bodies, is freed from bondage to decay.

Prior to this final act in God's redemptive work, it is God's love in Christ which sustains us, which empowers us—even in the midst of and in spite of our experiences of sin and death—"to be conformed to the image of his Son" (8:29). God works in all things toward that good purpose. But only "those who love him" know that, because they are participants "with him" in the outworking of that purpose.

• C H A P T E R 7 •

Is
God
Unjust?

Just as it is written: "Jacob I loved,
but Esau I hated." What then shall we say?
Is God unjust? Not at all! For he says
to Moses, "I will have mercy on whom I have mercy,
and I will have compassion on whom I have compassion."
ROMANS 9:13-15

Is God fair? Does he treat us unjustly? These natural human questions
are only magnified when we read passages like "Jacob I loved, but
Esau I hated" (Rom 9:13). Yet Paul himself wrestled with precisely this question as he reflected on Judaism's rejection of Christ
in light of Old Testament passages. What these Old Testament
passages, appealed to by Paul, seem to reveal is a sovereign arbitrariness in God's dealing with human beings. Statements like,
"Jacob I loved, but Esau I hated" provoke from us the question:
but why? What did they do to deserve either God's love or hate?
Our sense regarding some injustice here increases when we read
in 9:11 that decisions about Jacob and Esau were made "before

the twins were born or had done anything good or bad." Unfair! we are tempted to cry.

The "hardness" of this text arises at least in part both from assumptions which we tend to bring to it and our neglect regarding the flow and content of the surrounding text.

Paul anticipates the reader's response to the apparent injustice of God. In words reminiscent of those put to Job (Job 9:12; 40:2), he begins by questioning the appropriateness of even raising such questions (9:20). Then he drives home the point by citing Isaiah (29:16; 45:9): "Shall what is formed say to him who formed it, 'Why did you make me like this?' " (9:20-21).

Paul's point is, of course, that the question "Is God unjust?" arises from our human propensity to measure and critique God's ways *on our terms*. To even raise the question of unfairness assumes that we know what *fairness* in its final, absolute sense looks like. That is the creature's presumptuousness. Since we do not know the mind of God nor fathom his ways (Rom 11:33-34), we are not in a very good position to judge God's purposes. We see and experience only pieces; we see but poor reflections in a mirror and know only partially (1 Cor 13:12); we perceive God's revelation in the context of our earthen vessels (2 Cor 4:7). Only God sees the whole; and from that perspective what may seem "unjust" to us will finally be revealed as God's saving grace.

We bring another assumption to this text which skews our hearing of it in a particular direction. Because of certain theological traditions which are part of our legacy, we tend to hear this text in terms of predestination and eternal destiny. This theological tradition holds that our eternal destiny has been predetermined. The inevitable question to such a view is the one which Paul's hypothetical reader asks: "Then why does God still blame us? For who resists his will?" (9:19).

This question, when it comes from us, only has validity if Paul is in fact concerned here with the matter of individuals' eternal destiny. On close reading of the passage, however, it becomes clear that he is not speaking about salvation and eternal destiny, but about God's calling of individuals and peoples to service, and God's use of events and persons in the accomplishment of his redemptive purposes, namely the salvation of both Jews and Gentiles.

Let us attempt to hear Paul's argument clearly. He begins his consideration of the fate of his own people by recalling all that God had done for them and given them (9:1-5). The purpose of Israel's calling is that she be a vehicle for the realization of "the promise" (9:4, 8-9). For Paul, together with all of Judaism, this was a reference to the promise made to Abraham that through his descendants "all peoples on earth will be blessed" (Gen 12:1-3). Paul saw this promise as finding fulfillment in Christ (see Gal 3:15-18), through whose death both Jew and Gentile would be brought into God's family (Gal 3:28-29).

Yet the reality which Paul, and with him all Jewish Christians, faced was the rejection of Jesus by the people of Israel as a whole. Had God's word failed? (Rom 9:6). In answering this question, Paul shows, by reciting Old Testament events, that God chooses ways and means for accomplishing his redemptive purposes. And that even the present rejection of the Messiah by Israel is used by God toward that end. Not all the children of Abraham are part of the line which leads to the Christ. Isaac, the son promised to Sarah, becomes the vehicle (9:6-9). Jacob, not Esau, is used by God for moving toward the fulfillment of the promise (9:10-13). God's choices have nothing to do with human merit or status or achievement (9:11-12). Isaac was not better than his brother Ishmael; Jacob, not better than his brother Esau. In other words, they were not "more deserving." In fact, on purely human terms, Jacob's deception should have made him less deserving (Gen 25, 27).

At this point, Paul cites the prophetic word regarding Rebekah's unborn twins: "The older will serve the younger" (Gen 25:23). This is not so much a statement of predestination as of prophetic foreknowledge. The historical record reveals that when Israel's kingdom was strongest, Edom frequently was dominated by her and forced to pay tribute (2 Sam 8:13; 1 Kings 11:14-22). For Paul, confirmation for this prophecy regarding the future of Jacob and Esau (and their offspring) is found in Malachi 1:2-3, which he quotes in 9:13.

In the use of this word from Malachi about God's love for Jacob and hate for Esau, two things are to be noted. First, it is the prophet's concern to demonstrate God's love for Israel (Jacob's descendants), in order to go on to show that her unfaithfulness deserves God's judgment. The Edomites (Mal 1:4) are the descendants of Esau, who stand in a relationship of enmity with Israel. According to Malachi 1:3-4, they have apparently suffered military defeat, and the prophet sees this as evidence of God's judgment (1:4-5). Since God is using Israel to accomplish his purposes—despite her frequent rebellions—Edom's enmity sets it squarely against the purposes of God.

The expression "Jacob I loved, but Esau I hated" must be understood in this historical context. In contrast with God's obvious love for Israel, the situation of Edom could only be interpreted as evidence of God's lesser regard for it. The strong expression "Esau I hated" must be seen as a typical example of oriental hyperbole, which expresses things in terms of extremes. Further, in the Hebrew language "to love" often means "to favor"; and "to hate" can mean "to favor or to love less." Note, for example, that in Genesis 29:31, 33 the Revised Standard Version renders the Hebrew word *hate* literally, while the NIV renders the word with "not loved." That rendering recognizes, in light of Genesis 29:30, that Jacob loved Leah less than Rachel; he did not "hate" her. The more common meaning of "hate" is inappropriate here. (See also Deut 21:15-17, where the Hebrew word *hated* is rendered "not loved" in NIV and "disliked" in the RSV.)

Neither in Malachi, nor in Paul's use of it, is there then any warrant for the idea that God has determined in advance the eternal destinies of either Israel or Edom. Their historical situations, their "election" or "rejection," are but temporary evidences of God's sovereign freedom with which he moves history toward his redemptive purposes: "God so loved the world . . ." (Jn 3:16), including Jacob and Esau, Israel and Edom, Jew and Gentile.

This redemptive purpose is strongly underlined by Paul's citation of Exodus 33:19 at 9:15. God's mercy and compassion are absolutely free and at his sovereign disposal. No one can earn it; no one deserves it. Even the hardening of Pharaoh's heart, to which Paul refers in 9:17-18, is to be subsumed under the activity of God's mercy and compassion for his broken creation. For its purpose is that God's name "might be proclaimed in all the earth" (9:17). Thus, what from the limited vantage point of our human observation seems "unjust" is in fact only a misunderstanding of the mysterious workings of God's mercy.

· CHAPTER 8 ·

The End
of the
Law

*Christ is the end of the law
so that there may be righteousness
for everyone who believes.*
ROMANS 10:4

Romans 10:4, *though not the only place where Paul deals with the* law, raises more strongly than any other the question of the place of the law and its continuing validity for the Christian. This radical word about Christ as the end of the law—and similar expressions in other letters of Paul—have been the object of intense discussion throughout the history of the church, beginning as early as Paul's missionary journeys themselves. On the face of it, we are confronted with the affirmation that the law no longer determines our relationship with God. To the thinking of many, this has been a hard saying, which is open to the charge of *antinomianism*, the rejection of any and all laws and regulations, especially absolute norms, for the moral life.

Since the early church used the Jewish Scriptures as their Bible and included them in the canon together with the Gospels and other apostolic writings, the question of the relation between the law of God and Christian faith is an extremely important one.

In attempting to understand this text and its implications, we need to consider three things. First, Paul's understanding and experience of the law; second, his Damascus road experience as encounter with the Messiah of Jewish expectation; third, his new understanding of the law on the basis of the Christ event. Before we consider these three matters as a background for interpreting this text, a few words about Paul's use of the term *law* are in order.

Paul uses the term both in the figurative and literal sense. When he speaks of "a law in my members at war with the law of my mind" (Rom 7:23) or "the law of the Spirit of life" (Rom 8:2) or "the law of faith" (Rom 3:27), he is using the term figuratively to denote realities which are determinative for pagan or Christian life, like the Torah is determinative in the life of Israel. Apart from such usage, Paul only has the Mosaic law in view, that religious system with its cultic, ritualistic and moral obligations under which Israel lived its life since Moses. In this latter, literal sense, the term *law* in Romans 10:4 must be understood.

1. *Paul's understanding and experience of the law.* For Paul—"a Hebrew born of Hebrews, as to the law a Pharisee, as to righteousness under the law blameless" (Phil 3:5-6)—the law was God's law; it expressed God's will and purposes for God's people. To obey the law was to be obedient to the will of God. "The law is holy, and the commandment is holy and righteous and good" (Rom 7:12). It is "spiritual" (Rom 7:14) because it comes from God (Rom 7:22), and its intent is to lead human beings to real life (Rom 7:10).

As a rabbi, Paul knew very well that the law, as a gift of God's

grace, was a privilege to possess (Rom 9:4; 3:1-2). But he also
knew that this gift contained within it accountability. To "know
God's will," to "approve what is excellent," to be "instructed in
the law" (Rom 2:17-18)—and therefore to qualify as "a guide to
the blind, a light to those who are in darkness" (Rom 2:19)—also
meant that one was obligated to keep the law (Rom 2:17-24).

According to his own testimony, Paul believed that the keeping
of the law was possible. With regard to its obligation, he was
"blameless" (Phil 3:6). But that conviction was obliterated by his
experience of Christ.

2. *Paul's encounter with Christ.* Beginning with the Damascus
road experience—which Paul describes variously as that turning
point where God "was pleased to reveal his Son to me" (Gal 1:16)
or that event where "Christ Jesus has made me his own" (Phil
3:12)—Paul's understanding of the place and function of the law
underwent significant transformation. It had been his passionate
commitment to the law and the resultant zeal to uphold and
defend it which led him to persecute the early followers of Jesus.
There can be no doubt that he believed deeply that he was carrying out the will of God. But his encounter with the risen Lord
opened his eyes to see him as the Messiah of God. In his zeal for
the law he had actually opposed the purposes of God. He had
resisted the inbreaking of the messianic age (1 Cor 10:11) in the
very act of trying to keep the law.

This realization takes on particular force when it is seen
against the background of rabbinic views of history with which
Paul was likely familiar. Within that tradition some rabbis held
that human history was divided into three periods: (1) the period
of "chaos," lasting from Adam to Moses, when the law had not
been given; (2) the period of "Torah," lasting from Moses till the
Messiah, when the law would reign; (3) the period of the Messiah. Now regarding this last period there was considerable discussion among the rabbis about the place of the law. According

to some, the Torah was expected to cease in the messianic age; others held that the Messiah would perfect the law by giving it a new interpretation or that he would promulgate a new Torah.

Though the dominant thrust of the rabbinic tradition was that Torah would continue in and through the messianic age, that it was eternally valid, there are also many who thought there would be modifications, that some teachings would cease to be applicable, that others would acquire a new relevance, that the sacrificial system and the festivals would cease, that ceremonial distinctions between "clean" and "unclean" would no longer hold. Thus, a rabbinic tradition which both affirmed the continuance of the law in the messianic age and also recognized some form of cessation and/or modification forms the backdrop for Paul's experience and new understanding. The messianic age had dawned. The Torah could no longer be seen as before.

In addition to this rabbinic tradition, the attitude of Jesus himself to the law must have had some impact on Paul's thinking. Though we cannot know to what extent Paul was informed about the precise content of Jesus' teaching and actions, the general stance of Jesus with regard to the law was surely part of the traditions which Paul received from his predecessors in the faith. And that stance contains elements which provide both continuity and discontinuity with common Jewish perceptions about the law.

According to Matthew 5:17, Jesus came not to abolish the law. Throughout the couplets which follow ("You have heard that it was said, . . . but I say to you") it is clear that Jesus affirms the eternal validity of God's will as expressed in the law, but that he also drives his hearers to the deepest and most comprehensive meaning of that will by transcending traditional and often limiting interpretations of the law. As Messiah he provides authoritative interpretation.

Further, according to both Matthew 5:17-18 and the witness of the Gospels and the earliest Christian preaching, Jesus "fulfilled the law" in his life, death and resurrection. He is declared as the fulfillment of Scripture. In him, the purposes of God are accomplished. This general conviction is undergirded by the authoritative, sovereign way in which Jesus deals with specific and limiting dimensions of the law and sets his mission on a level of significance above the law. Thus, laws of separation between clean and unclean, of ceremonial defilement, of sabbath observance, are set aside in the pursuit of his ministry to sinners and ritually (ceremonially) "unclean" persons. The "law and the prophets were until John," he said (Mt 11:13; Lk 16:16), indicating that a new reality, the messianic kingship, had entered the scene and was replacing the old order (Mk 1:15).

With this background in focus, it is perhaps easier to grasp both the continuity and discontinuity between Paul's thinking about the law and that of his rabbinic contemporaries.

3. *Paul's new understanding of the law.* Paul reflects acquaintance with the rabbinic discussion about the three periods of human history. But on the basis of his own experience of Christ and Jesus' own stance toward the law, Paul intensifies and explicates particularly that strand of the tradition which either envisaged a cessation of the law or at least its transformation in the third or messianic period. He saw Jesus as having "abolished in his flesh the law with its commandments and ordinances" (Eph 2:15). Through him "we are discharged from the law" which once "held us captive" (Rom 7:6).

Serving "under the old written code" (Rom 7:6) and seeking to establish his own righteousness (Rom 10:3) had only brought Paul into opposition to the very purpose of God rather than into peace with God. In Romans 7 he shows that the law as expression of God's will remains; that it reveals, as ever, human sin and rebellion against God. But he also shows that the law is powerless to bring about obedience. It is an external norm; it does not provide the power with which to achieve the norm. Therefore the attempt to achieve "righteousness based on the law" (Rom 10:5) invariably ends in the experience of failure. Paul's summation of this experience is caught up in the words: "Wretched man that I am, who will deliver me" (Rom 7:24).

His answer to that question is "Jesus Christ my Lord" (Rom 7:25). Why? Because "Christ is the end of the law." The word *end* (*telos*) can designate either the "goal," "outcome," "purpose" toward which something is directed, or the "end," "cessation." Many interpreters believe that both meanings are caught up in our text. For Paul, the law "was our custodian until Christ came" (Galatians 3:24). Its temporary function has now been accomplished; and Christ is therefore also the terminus, the cessation of the law.

But Paul is saying much more here than simply repeating the conviction of one aspect of his tradition and the witness of the early church that there is a cessation of the law in the messianic period. He qualifies the conviction that the Mosaic law has been completed and abrogated in Christ with the phrase "unto righteousness." Our English translations have not served us well here, for they have generally blunted the connection between the statement "Christ is the end of the law" and the qualifying phrase "unto righteousness."

The preposition *unto* expresses purpose or goal. Christ is not the end of the law in an absolute sense. He does not abolish the will of God as expressed in the law. Rather his coming signals its end with regard to the attainment of righteousness (that is, right relationship with God). He is the revelation of God's righteousness (Rom 1:17). His life is an incarnation of God's relation-restoring action, God's way of setting us right (Rom 10:3). Therefore, the law as a means of approach to God, as that which determines relationship with God, as that which was perceived in Paul's Jewish tradition to lead to life on the basis of conformity, has been abolished.

A third phrase in our text adds a further qualifier to the assertion that Christ is the end of the law. Namely, he is the end of the law "for everyone who believes." For it is only in the response of faith to Christ, in the humble submission to God's righteousness (Rom 10:3) that the bondage of the law—consisting of its revelation of sin and its inability to help us beyond it—can come to its end.

· C H A P T E R 9 ·

Israel's
Salvation

---

*And so all Israel
will be saved.*
ROMANS 11:26

A ll Israel will be saved?" Does this mean every single Jew, or Israel
as a national entity? Didn't Judaism on the whole reject Christ
and thus refuse God's saving act? How then can "all Israel" be
saved? And didn't Jesus, before Paul, say that the kingdom of
God would be taken away from the Jewish people and given to
a new people (Mt 21:43)?

Romans 11:26 has been at the heart of much Christian reflection about eschatology or doctrines about end times. I remember
well the interpretation given this text by one of my college
teachers. According to his eschatological timeline, the establish-
ment of the State of Israel in 1948, which ended an almost 2000-

year period without nationhood, inaugurated the final days of
"the time of the Gentiles," namely that period when the land of
Israel was occupied by Gentiles. (Compare Lk 21:24, where Jesus
predicts the destruction of Jerusalem and a subsequent period of
its being "trodden down by the Gentiles until the times of the
Gentiles are fulfilled.")

But since 1948, so said our teacher, there is one piece of the
eschatological puzzle still missing: the Old City of Jerusalem was
still being held by the Arabs. The State of Israel only held the
new city. A barbed-wire fence separated Jews from their ancient
city, including the Temple mount. When that fence comes down
and Israel regains control over the Old City, so our teacher con-
fidently predicted, Jerusalem will no longer be "trodden down by
the Gentiles." Thus, "the times of the Gentiles will be fulfilled"
and the conversion of Israel to its Messiah will be inaugurated.
Many of us who took this and other very specific eschatological
views seriously waited expectantly when, during the 1967 Arab-
Israeli War, the fence did come down and Israel regained control
over its ancient city. Over twenty years have passed, but Israel
has remained a thoroughly secular state.

This rather recent historical experience illustrates the precar-
ious nature of all eschatological theories which tie particular biblical texts to very specific historical events. It also reveals the
difficulty of understanding the precise meaning of Paul's word
that "all Israel will be saved." In order to gain a clearer perspective on this matter, we will examine Paul's extended discussion
with regard to Israel in Romans 9—11 with particular focus on
the immediate context of Romans 11:11-27.

After showing that God's redemptive action in and through
Christ (Rom 1—4) has brought freedom from condemnation
(Rom 5), sin (Rom 6), law (Rom 7) and death (Rom 8), Paul brings
this part of his letter to a climax with a magnificent description
of God's love in Christ from which nothing can separate us. This

glorious doxology is abruptly overshadowed in 9:1-2 by an expression of Paul's deep pain over the fact that Israel, the people of God, had rejected their Messiah.

The question of Israel's fate, in light of its rejection of the early Christian proclamation that Jesus of Nazareth was the fulfillment of Israel's prophetic hope, was very much in the consciousness of Jewish followers of the risen Christ. A sense of perplexity and incredulity regarding Jewish unbelief is reflected throughout the New Testament, beginning with the Gospels. But for Paul, it must have been particularly intense. Had not he, a leader of the opposition to this messianic faith, been grasped from the darkness of unbelief to the light and freedom of faith in Christ? But beyond this personal dimension, were not his people those who had been the objects of God's gracious activity through the calling of father Abraham, the creation of a nation, the deliverance of the exodus, the giving of law and covenant? Had not they been the objects of God's steadfast love and faithfulness from which "nothing can separate," as he had just confessed in 8:31? If the word of God does not fail (9:6), why is Israel stuck in the failure of disobedience? That is the agonizing question which Paul addresses in Romans 9—11.

After the opening lament over Israel (9:1-5), Paul proceeds to show in a variety of ways that God's redemptive purposes, inaugurated with the call of Abraham and brought to a climax in Christ, have in fact not failed, even with regard to the people of Israel.

He begins by demonstrating that from the very beginning belonging to the people of God was not a matter of birthright (vv. 7-8) nor of human achievement (vv. 11, 16). Rather, membership in God's family is determined solely by the promise (v. 8), calling (v. 11) and mercy (v. 16) of God. In this context, Paul introduces a different use of the term *Israel* which he has already indicated earlier in this epistle (see 2:28-29; see also Gal 3:7; 6:16); namely, there is an Israel "of the flesh" and an Israel "of the promise." Both are determined by the gracious action of God, but the latter transcends the boundaries of the former. That "the children of God" (v. 8) have their existence purely on the basis of God's calling and mercy is underlined by the analogy of the potter and the clay in verses 19-23. The potter is sovereign over the clay. And, in that sovereignty, he has called into peoplehood both a remnant from the people of Israel and from the Gentiles (v. 24). The citation of prophetic words from Hosea and Isaiah (vv. 25-26) underlines this fact.

In the following section (9:30-10:4), Paul goes on to state why the redemptive purposes of God are being received and realized among the Gentiles and why Israel as a whole is rejecting them. Israel rejected the righteousness of God—his relation-restoring action which culminated in the servant-ministry of Jesus—because it sought to establish its own righteousness by external conformity to the law. This attempt to secure one's own worth and standing with God—which, according to Paul's earlier discussion in this epistle (2:17-29), invariably results in boasting and self-righteousness—leads to refusal to submit to God's way (10:3). And God's way is that as creature we respond to the love and faithfulness of the Creator with faith, that we believe his Word, that we respond in trust (10:5-13).

The opportunity to respond to God in this way has been there throughout Israel's history, as Paul demonstrates by reference to Old Testament texts (10:14-21). And throughout that history, including the coming of God's righteousness in the Messiah, Israel has been "a disobedient and contrary people" (10:21).

Does this history of rejection and disobedience mean that God has finally thrown in the towel on his people Israel? That is the question which occupies Paul in the next section of the epistle (11:1-10). The answer to the question is no. For just as God called out a remnant from a disobedient nation in the past (vv. 2-4), so too there is a remnant in the present which has responded in faith to God's grace (v. 5). Paul himself is evidence of the existence of such a remnant within Judaism (11:1).

But the fact remains that the vast majority of Israel has refused to submit to God's way of salvation by finally rejecting his Messiah. True enough. But God is not yet done with his people. Though Paul has been very adamant throughout the epistle that faith and belonging to Christ are the only criteria for what it means to be "of the seed of Abraham" (2:20; 9:6-8), Paul also decidedly rejects the idea that this truth means the exclusion of the nation of Israel from God's redemptive purposes (the analogy of the olive tree in 11:17-24 underlines that). For him, such a conclusion would have been inconsistent with the historical election of Israel (see 11:29).

Thus Paul acknowledges Israel's failure and rejection (11:7), but he proceeds to argue that within God's overarching purposes this reality is temporally limited. Indeed, God uses the present rejection for his purposes. This activity of God is underscored by the Scripture citations from Isaiah 29 and Psalm 69 about the hardening of Israel (11:8-10), for since Israel's disobedience is placed in the service of God's purpose, God can be spoken of as "hardening" Israel. But the goal of disobedience and hardening is not their ultimate rejection and destruction (11:11); it is, rather, twofold: (1) the salvation of the Gentiles (the world) and (2) the ultimate salvation of Israel (11:11-15).

Paul is convinced that through the proclamation of the gospel to the Gentiles and its acceptance by them, the promise to Abraham—that all the people of the earth shall be blessed in him—is being fulfilled (see Rom 4). He is also convinced, on the basis of Deuteronomy 32:21, which he cites in 10:19, that the salvation of the Gentiles will provoke Israel to jealousy and open them to the gospel (11:11, 14).

Within the context of this argument (11:11-16), Paul anticipates the "mystery" regarding the nation of Israel's ultimate destiny, which he articulates in our "hard saying" later in 11:25-26. If, as he argues in 11:12, the failure of Israel is leading to the salvation of the Gentiles, the manifestation of God's grace and blessing will be ever so much greater with "their full inclusion." What does he mean with this expression?

The term translated "full inclusion" in the RSV text is the Greek word *plērōma*. The ASV renders this term by "fulfillment" or "fullness." In 11:25, the same expression is used again, but this time in connection with the Gentiles. Here RSV renders it as "full number of the Gentiles," while ASV renders "fullness of the Gentiles." I am persuaded that the idea of a divinely predetermined number, which has to be made up both of Gentiles and Jews, is not within Paul's purview here. When noncanonical Jewish apocalyptic literature speaks of a "full number" of Israelites in relation to end events, the word used is not *plērōma* but *arithmos*. In Revelation, we read of "the number of the sealed" in 7:4. The word used, just as in the Jewish apocalyptic literature, is not *plērōma* but *arithmos*, and the number is generally regarded as symbolic rather than indicative of numerical extent. Thus we do better to seek the meaning for Paul's use of *plērōma* in his use of the term elsewhere in his writings.

With but one exception (Rom 13:10), the most natural rendering of Paul's use of *plērōma* is "fullness" or "completeness" (Rom 15:29; Gal 4:4; Eph 1:23; 3:19; 4:13; Col 1:19, 2:9). What then do the expressions "Israel's fullness" (11:12) and "the fullness of the Gentiles" (11:25) mean? Light may be shed on this problem by Paul's use of verbal cognates of *plērōma* in three texts where his mission to the Gentiles is in focus. In Romans 15:18-22 he speaks of having "fully preached" the gospel of Christ to the Gentiles and now being desirous of expanding this mission to Spain. In Colossians 1:25-27 he speaks of having made the "word of God fully known" among the Gentiles. And in 2 Timothy 4:17 he confesses God's empowerment "to proclaim the message fully, that all the Gentiles might hear."

In light of these usages, Johannes Munck argues convincingly, in his book *Christ and Israel*, that Paul's commitment to the full dissemination of the gospel to the Gentiles must provide the interpretive key to his use of *plērōma* in 11:12 and 11:25. The expression "the fullness [or completion] of the Gentiles" in 11:25 then denotes the final result of Paul's proclamation of the gospel to the Gentiles. God's purpose through that preaching is their salvation, their completion (as children of God in Christ; see Col 2:10).

The completion of the mission to the Gentiles will result in, or lead to, Israel's "fullness" or "completion" (11:12), her "acceptance" (11:15). These phrases anticipate the affirmation in 11:26 that "all Israel will be saved." The way from the anticipation of this conviction to this climactic expression is paved by the analogy of the olive tree (11:17-24) and its astounding claim that God will indeed graft the broken-off branches of unbelieving Israel back into the olive tree to join the branches of "remnant Jews" and believing Gentiles who have already been grafted to the olive tree.

Paul proclaims this future realization of God's intention as "a mystery" (11:25). He is not referring here to a special revelation which he received, some esoteric secret communicated to him directly in a vision or dream. Rather, he is referring to God's redemptive action and purpose, revealed in the life, death and resurrection of Christ which he proclaims (Rom 16:25; 1 Cor 2:1-2; Eph 6:16; Col 2:2, where "God's mystery" is simply identified as "Christ"). Sometimes, as in our text, the term is used more specifically for God's plan of salvation. The most instructive parallel to our text—which envisions the grafting of both Gentile and Jew into the same olive tree—is Ephesians 3:3-6, where Paul says that the content of the "mystery of Christ" is the inclusion of the Gentiles as fellow heirs of the promise with Jews in the new community of Christ's body.

Within this overarching content of the mystery which Paul proclaims is a more specific component. Namely, that the "hardening which has come upon part of Israel" (11:25) is limited not only in extent, but also with regard to time: its rejection will last only "until the fullness of the Gentiles comes." This completion of God's purpose among the Gentiles leads then to the completion of that same redemptive purpose for Israel (11:12), in that "all Israel will be saved" (11:26). Commentators are agreed that "all Israel" means Israel "as a whole," as a historical people who have a unique and particular identity, not necessarily including every individual Israelite. Support for this way of understanding the phrase "all Israel" comes from a rabbinic tract (Sanhedrin X, 1), where the statement "all Israelites have a share in the world to come" is immediately qualified by a list of exceptions, such as the Sadducees, heretics, magicians, and so on. The salvation of Israel is comprehensive, but not all-inclusive. In our text, just as "the fullness of the Gentiles" does not mean that each individual Gentile will "believe in his heart and confess with his lips" (10:10), so the "fullness of Israel" cannot mean every individual Jew.

While in 11:25-26 the present "part of Israel" which is hardened is contrasted with "all Israel" which will be saved in the future, it is clear that "all Israel" denotes both the already-saved remnant and the yet-to-be-saved "rest" (11:7). What is also clear from the whole thrust of the discussion in Romans 9—11 is that God's purposes for the salvation of Israel will be realized in no other way and by no other means than through the preaching of the gospel and the response of faith. It is that preaching and that response which will lead to "life from the dead" (11:15), clearly a reference to the eschatological event of the resurrection which will be preceded by the "completion of Israel" (11:26) as the last stage in the process initiated by the death and resurrection of Jesus.

In light of where we began this chapter, a final observation is important. There is no indication anywhere in these chapters of Romans that Paul has in view the conversion of Israel as a nation-state, located on a particular piece of real estate. Already in Paul's time, there were more Jews living outside Palestine than within. What Paul does envision is a time when the gospel will be heard and accepted by his people as a whole, scattered throughout the world but, nonetheless, a unique, identifiable people whose identity is rooted in the great historical events of redemptive history and whose future is guaranteed by the God who has saved his people and will again save them by "banishing ungodliness" and "taking away their sins" (11:26-27).

CHAPTER 10

God Has Bound All to Disobedience

For God has bound all men
over to disobedience so that
he may have mercy on them all.
ROMANS 11:32

If God has bound all human beings to disobedience (or, as the RSV
translates, "consigned all men to disobedience"), where does human responsibility lie? How can God hold us responsible for
disobedience when God caused it? The text seems clearly to indicate that the disobedience of both Jews and Gentiles (11:30-31)
is in some sense the activity of God *so that* his mercy can be
demonstrated. An analogy will highlight the "hardness" of this
text. In order to demonstrate my heroic nature, I push a non-
swimmer into a swift current. As he is about to drown, I jump
in and save him. Is such a view of God's ways a valid understanding of Paul's words?

An answer to this problem depends largely on the meaning of the Greek word rendered "bound over to disobedience," and our understanding of Paul's general view of God's relation to human sinfulness or disobedience.

That the Greek word used by Paul is open to a range of meanings and nuances is clear from the following list of a representative sample of English versions:

NIV	has bound over to disobedience
ASV	has shut up unto disobedience
KJV	hath concluded them in unbelief
NEB	making all prisoners to disobedience
Berkeley	confined under the power of disobedience
Jerusalem	imprisoned in their own disobedience
TEV	has made prisoners to disobedience

The Greek word reflected in these translations is *synkleiō*. In the standard Greek-English Lexicon by Bauer/Arndt/Gingrich, both literal and figurative meanings are given. The literal meaning of the verb is "close up together," "hem in," "enclose." That meaning is clearly present in Luke 5:6, where a catch of fish is "enclosed" in a net. The figurative meaning is given as "confine, imprison," and illustrated from Romans 11:32. The word's possible meanings in this text are then given as follows: *"he has imprisoned them all in disobedience,* i.e. put them under compulsion to be disobedient or given them over to disobedience." The sense of "compulsion" by God is reflected strongly in the renderings of TEV, ASV, NEB. The alternative meaning, "given them over," is reflected in the translation of the Jerusalem Bible.

In the New Testament, apart from its literal use in Luke 5:6 and our text, *synkleiō* is used in only one other Pauline text, Galatians 3:22-23. Here Paul affirms that "Scripture declares that the whole world is a prisoner to sin" (v. 22). That state of bondage to sin is paralleled by the statement in verse 23 that "we were held prisoners by the law."

The meaning of *synkleiō* in this text is certainly that of confinement (or restraint, as in RSV). Yet God is not seen as determining that bondage in any direct way. The meaning of verse 22 seems to be that Scripture shows—by virtue of the history of human disobedience since the Fall—that all are in the grip of sin. The reference to confinement under the law in verse 23 must be interpreted in light of verses 24-25, where the function of the law is put in very positive terms: it is the custodial caretaker, leading us to Christ. What is confirmed in this passage's use of *synkleiō* is the reality of bondage to sin or disobedience, as expressed in 12:32. But the possibility of God as determiner of human disobedience does not seem to be in view.

Help for grasping Paul's meaning may be found in the Old Testament as well as in Romans 1. The Hebrew Scriptures had been translated into Greek in the centuries before Jesus' coming, and Paul made frequent use of this translation when he cited, or referred to, those Scriptures.

The Hebrew word *sagar*, which means "to deliver up," "to surrender," "to give over," is translated in the Greek Old Testament by two different words. In Psalm 31:8 and 78:50 the translators used *synkleiō*. In Psalm 78:48 and Deuteronomy 32:30, the same Hebrew word was represented by the Greek *paradidōmi*.

It is clear from this and many other examples which could be given that for the Greek translators these Greek words were both valid equivalents for the Hebrew *sagar*, if not synonymous. Kittel's *Theological Dictionary of the New Testament* states that *synkleiō*, as a translation of *sagar*, means "to deliver up," "to surrender"; and that it is parallel to *paradidōmi*.

It is this latter word which Paul uses in Romans 1:24, 26, 28. In 1:18-32, as in 11:32, Paul stresses the pervasiveness and depth of human sin. Its origin is the human refusal to acknowledge God as God (Rom 1:18-23). Paul then goes on to show that in the context of this rejection of God, human life deteriorates and degenerates (1:24-32). This depiction of human sinfulness is accompanied by the threefold refrain "therefore, God gave them over to" (RSV "gave them up"). The meaning is clearly that God allowed his creation to sink in the quicksand of its own disobedience. He neither forced its obedience, nor determined its disobedience.

With these insights we are now able to return to our text in Romans 11:23. Paul's use of the word *synkleiō* should best be understood in keeping with its usage in the Greek Old Testament where, in translation of the Hebrew *sagar*, it means "to deliver up," "to surrender." This sense of the term is confirmed, as we have seen, by the use of the parallel word in Romans 1:24-28. The meaning of 12:32 would then be: "God has given up all people to their disobedience." What we have here then is an expression of God's permissive will. By permitting the creation to become absorbed in and by its sinfulness, God has acted in such a way that the result is their bondage in disobedience. It is that bondage which is the object of God's liberating grace.

CHAPTER 11

Heaping
Burning
Coals

If your enemy is hungry, feed him;
if he is thirsty, give him something
to drink. In doing this,
you will heap burning coals on his head.
ROMANS 12:20

The *image of pouring burning coals on another's head—even though* we realize that it is a figure of speech—conjures up negative connotations. It sounds like vengeance or retribution. Surely that is not the result to be achieved by acts of kindness. Could Paul be saying that doing good to one's enemies is an indirect way of punishing them?

These negative assessments disappear rather quickly when we see this passage in its larger context (both in Rom 12 and in Prov 25:21-22, from where it is cited) and properly grasp the meaning of this figure of speech in its ancient Near Eastern setting.

The entire context argues against the possibility of interpret-

ing this figure in a negative sense. As a whole, Romans 12 begins
the final section of the epistle in which Paul, on the basis of his
theology of justification by faith and the empowering of Christian life by the Spirit, works out some of the practical implications of this theology for everyday Christian existence. He begins by speaking of the transformation of life in such a way that
God's good will is accomplished in and through Christians (vv.
1-2). He continues by showing that as Christians we do not stand
alone in this task, but are one body, gifted by God's grace to
empower each other in mutual loving service (vv. 3-13). Then he
focuses on Christians' existence in the larger world, a world
which, for the early believers, was often hostile toward the followers of Christ (vv. 14-21).

In such a world, it would have been very natural and easy to
build resentment, to lash out, to resort to even violent means in
order to protect oneself against hostility and persecution. But
Paul knew, on the basis of Jesus' "suffering servant" Messiah-
ship, that the way of bitterness, resentment and violence was not
to be the way of Jesus' followers in this world. God's love, demonstrated in Jesus' death on the cross and poured into believers'
hearts (Rom 5:5), was stronger than hate. He had experienced its
grasp on his life while he was a persecutor of Christians (see Phil
3:4-12).

The proper response to those who persecute is to bless, not
curse, them (12:14). The evil done to you should not be repaid
by evil (12:17). In situations of conflict, Christians ought to be
about the search for peace (12:18). Where the world's values
would call for retribution and vengeance when evil is done to us,
we are, on the contrary, to respond in love and kindness, going
as far as giving food and drink to enemies who are hungry and
thirsty (12:19-20). Why? Because God is the one who judges and
holds evildoers responsible in the final judgment (12:19). When
we respond to evil in the radically unexpected form of goodness,

we are in effect pouring "burning coals" on the head of the per-
petrator of evil (12:20). Paul drives home this radical Christian
response to evil, urging that we refuse to "overcome by evil," but
instead "overcome evil with good" (12:21).

Verse 21, in confirmation of the entire context of the passage,
demonstrates that the figure of "pouring burning coals" is to be
understood as an act of goodness, as something which "over-
comes evil with good." This meaning of the figure is confirmed
even by the context of our figure in Proverbs 25:21-22, which
closes with the words, "and the Lord will reward you." And in
the Old Testament, God's rewards are always seen as response
to human acts of kindness.

This analysis of the context shows that the image of burning
coals must have a positive meaning. It does not tell us precisely
what that meaning is, what "pouring burning coals" on an enemy's head is to accomplish. To that question we now turn.

Romans 12:2 implies that the "burning coals" image refers to
an "overcoming" of evil. How is the evil of the enemy overcome?
Help in answering this question comes from both biblical (internal) and nonbiblical (external) sources. In the narrative of the
prophet Isaiah's call (Is 6), the recognition of his sinfulness receives a divine response of purging and purification. A burning
coal is taken from the altar and applied to his mouth, with the
assurance that "your guilt is taken away, and your sin forgiven"
(Is 6:7). This connection between burning coals and repentance
and cleansing is also present (though not as directly) in Malachi's
picture of God as one who is "like a refiner's fire" (Mal 3:2). As
fire refines silver and gold to purify it, so God will "purify the
sons of Levi . . . till they present right offerings to the LORD"
(Mal 3:3 RSV). The point of this passage is that Israel's sin and
disobedience shall be separated out through the refining process
of God's judgment.

A possible cultural background, outside the Bible, for the connection between burning coals/fire and the purging of sin/evil is to be seen in the ancient Egyptian custom in which a penitent demonstrated his repentance of a wrong committed by carrying a dish of burning coals on his head. Some commentators see this as the immediate background of the proverb which Paul cites (Prov 25:21-22).

In light of the above discussion, the purpose of "pouring burning coals" seems to be that, by means of responding to evil with good, the doer of the evil may be brought to repentance. It is the enemy's benefit which is intended. When the adversary is treated with kindness, when good is returned for evil, then evil may be overcome; the antagonist may be transformed by a renewal of mind, a change of orientation from darkness to light.

• C H A P T E R   1 2 •

Submitting
to
Government

Everyone must submit himself
to the governing authorities,
for there is no authority except that
which God has established.
ROMANS 13:1

How do Christians deal with the tension created by their presence
in a society in which the need to preserve their integrity as individuals and to be faithful to their understanding of the lordship
of Christ may conflict with the demands of that society?

In Romans 13 Paul focuses on the tension between the individual and society at large in terms of the problem of civil obedience or disobedience. The question which is raised concerns the
individual's responsibility toward the social order, insofar as that
social order is regulated by laws which are upheld and enforced
by government authorities.

Individual Christian responsibility has often been compromised on the basis of a one-sided use of biblical injunctions. Thus Romans 13 and 1 Peter 2:13-14 are often cited as proof that the state always demands and deserves our total and unquestioning obedience. But Revelation 13 and 18 are neglected. The former pictures the state as a beast opposed to God's purposes; the latter speaks of the downfall of any nation which becomes a modern Babylon, corrupted by its wealth, materialism and injustice.

Some Christians are quick to condemn any person who upsets or threatens to upset social norms and regulations. But those same Christians tend to disregard Acts 17:6-7 where the apostles are described as "men who have turned the world upside down" and who "are all acting against the decrees of Caesar, saying that there is another king, Jesus."

The Gospel accounts also make clear that Jesus did not accept all legal and governing authorities as ultimate dispensers of God's will. Wherever he went, he bucked the system, he upset the status quo, he challenged the authorities' claim to the right and the truth. And in the context of a life of discipleship, countless martyrs have given their lives because they resisted the decrees of the authorities.

Thus a serious look at the scriptural material will prevent us from viewing the demands of society and its rulers with uncritical acceptance and automatic approval. Are there conditions when the demands of the social order must be resisted and the worth of the individual as a responsible being before God must be affirmed and defended?

If we cannot give uncritical and unquestioning allegiance to the demands of society and its governing authorities, we must also be careful not to go to the other extreme, that of concluding that government is inevitably an evil institution which should be resisted, disobeyed, distrusted or ignored. For we are instructed to honor and pray for those in authority. The Bible makes clear that government has a positive role to play in God's plans for human community. According to the New Testament, all authority is ultimately under the rule and judgment of Christ.

In light of this double perspective, how are we to understand Romans 13, which seems to come down on one side of this double perspective? First, we need to read Romans 13 more carefully than it has often been read. Second, we need to read these admonitions in light of the context of Paul's missionary activity, which took place in a world in which Roman law and rule had created relative peace and order, conducive to the rapid spread of the gospel.

Let us carefully follow, in outline form, Paul's argument:

Statement: "Let every person be subject to the governing authorities" (13:1).

Hypothetical Question: Why?

Answer: Because all authority exists ultimately by God's design, including the authority of the state (13:1).

Conclusion: Therefore, to resist the authorities is to resist God's intent (13:2).

Hypothetical Question: But what is God's intent?

Answer: It is God's intent that through his "servants" (governing authorities) evil acts are punished (13:4); bad works are restrained through fear of punishment (13:3); and the good is promoted and encouraged (13:3).

In summary, Paul's argument is this: It is God's intent that human life in the context of community will be life in harmony and peace and order (see 12:10, 18). Since life in community becomes chaotic and anarchistic without the presence of regulatory laws which are enforced by authorities, the presence of these are part of God's overall intent for human existence. Therefore, insofar as the state and its rulers exercise their authority in keeping with God's intent, they act as God's ministers for the common good of society.

If, however, the authority of the state runs counter to this divine intent, then that authority should not be understood as God-given. In fact, it becomes quite clear from Revelation 13 and 18, as well as other places in the New Testament, that the state which persecutes Christians, which dispenses injustice instead of justice, which supports moral decay, which tramples on the weak and powerless, has been usurped by demonic powers and forces which are diametrically opposed to God's intents and purposes.

The passage which follows Paul's discussion about the relationship between the individual and the demands of the social order (13:8-10) is very instructive for a proper understanding of that relationship. Most commentators feel that Paul has completed the considerations about obedience to the state (13:1-7) and is now speaking about morality and ethics in general. It seems to me, however, that such an understanding of the thrust of the argument overlooks Paul's specific intent at this point.

Indeed, the admonitions concerning love for others (13:8-10) are not a departure from the previous topic, but are rather a climax of the entire discussion. Verse 8 picks up very pointedly from verse 7. There the argument for obedience to the state and for responsible existence within the social order is driven home in terms of specific things that we owe: taxes, respect, honor. But beyond these specifics, Paul goes on to argue (vv. 8-9) that what we really owe is to love others even as we love ourselves.

According to Paul's Jewish heritage, government authorities are intended to be guardians of the commandments which make community life possible. The commandments, "do not kill," "do not steal," "do not commit adultery," and so forth, if violated, lead to the destruction and fragmentation of community. Since the law is summed up in the command "You shall love your neighbor as yourself" (v. 9), the loving of one's fellow human beings—not doing any wrong to them—"is the fulfilling of the law" (v. 10). It is responsibility for both the protection and the enforcing of this law which is given to human authorities by God's design.

What if, in our expression of love to our fellow human beings, we run smack into the laws of the society in which we live? What if the rulers act in opposition to their intended purpose as stated in 13:3? What if they become "a terror to the good"? What if the demands of the social order require us to be molded into a lifestyle which is contrary to the implicit and explicit demands of the gospel?

There are no pat answers to these questions. Anyone who suggests easy solutions or indeed *the* Christian response fails to take seriously the complexities of the world in which we find ourselves. Nonetheless, we must be sensitive to the issues raised by these questions and must respond in keeping with our understanding of the call of Christ. And that call is decisively a call to be there for others in love. If we fail at this point, even the most carefully woven cloth of orthodox belief and pious practice will finally become nothing but a tattered rag.

· C H A P T E R 1 3 ·

Eating
That
Destroys

If your brother is distressed
because of what you eat, you are
no longer acting in love.
Do not by your eating destroy your
brother for whom Christ died.
ROMANS 14:15

Romans 14:15, *together with the related texts in 1 Corinthians 8* and 10, contains what has often been called the "stumbling block" principle. It is the principle of Christian life and conduct which holds that whatever we do or say should not become a hindrance to the faith and life of a Christian brother or sister.

The difficulty which this principle has created for many Christians is not so much related to understanding its import, but rather its implementation. What guidance does the apostle give in this regard? How can we know whether what we eat (or drink or wear or participate in) merely offends fellow Christians and is rejected as inappropriate by them, or causes fellow Christians to stumble and fall in their faith-pilgrimage and perhaps even reject the faith?

These are precisely the issues with which Paul deals in Romans 14. We shall carefully trace his argument, completing that investigation with insights from 1 Corinthians, where Paul struggles with similar concerns.

In the previous chapters of this epistle (Romans 12—13), Paul has laid down central principles for Christian conduct, both within the community of the church and in the larger world of human relationships. Within the fellowship, we are to be more concerned with others than with ourselves (12:3, 10). In the larger human society, we are to respond to evil with good (12:14) and thus overcome the evil (12:21). Both of these "principles" for Christian conduct are undergirded by the most central principle: "Love does no harm to the neighbor. Therefore love is the fulfillment of the law" (13:10).

It is this principle with which Paul now confronts a problem that was very acute in several of the young churches. For Gentile Christians, the issue was whether they could eat meat that was sold in the open marketplace, but which had come from animals sacrificed in heathen temples. It was a very concrete problem in the context of their continuing social relationships with heathen neighbors and friends. For Jewish Christians, in the context of fellowship with Gentile Christians, there was the tension between Jewish ceremonial laws regarding "clean" and "unclean" foods and the freedom of Gentile believers from those regulations. We see early Jewish Christians struggling with that issue in the Acts accounts of Peter's vision (Acts 10) and of the Jerusalem Council (Acts 15).

Most likely Paul wrote Romans from Corinth. Thus his views about the issues facing believers in Rome would surely have been informed by the way he treated this matter in the church in Corinth. There (1 Cor 8, 10) he talks about the "weak," those who are young in the faith, whose consciences are tender, who are still prone, due to their heathen background, to make the link between the idol and the meat sacrificed to the idol. The "strong" are those who know, who are clearly convinced that idols (and the gods they represent) have no real existence. For them, therefore, meat offered to these gods in sacrifice is neutral. One cannot be defiled by it. The "strong" are clearly "correct" in their theology; the "weak" are definitely "wrong." And yet, Paul argues, those who have correct knowledge should take care that their knowledge does not lead to the ruin of a brother or sister (1 Cor 8:7-9). For the freedom of the "strong" with regard to this matter may lead the "weak" to return to the sphere of idolatry (1 Cor 8:10-13; 10:23-32).

We must recognize that Paul is not concerned here about simply offending others by doing something with which they disagree, or which they deem inappropriate or unacceptable for Christians. Rather, he is concerned about the eternal welfare of these "weak" Christians, about acts which cause them to fall in their spiritual journey, leading to the destruction of their young faith (8:9, 11-13; 10:32).

The principles which Paul lays down are identical to those given in Romans 12—13: Do nothing that causes fellow believers to come to ruin (8:13; 10:32); rather, build them up in love (8:1); seek the good of others (10:24, 33).

With this background from the Corinthian situation, we are now ready to follow Paul's similar argument in Romans 14. There the "weak" seem to be Jewish Christians, who have not yet been able to become free from the ritual and ceremonial laws concerning clean or unclean foods (10:1-6) or the observance of special days (probably a reference to Sabbath observance—10:5). The majority who stand in tension with the weak are most likely Gentile Christians, for whom there is no such thing as "unclean foods" or special days to be observed.

Their conflict with each other apparently manifested itself in
an attitude of haughtiness or spiritual superiority by the Gentile
believers and a condemning, judgmental spirit toward them by
Jewish believers (14:3-4, 10, 13). Paul comes down hard on both
for three reasons: (1) God has already accepted both (14:3); (2)
we are ultimately accountable in these matters to God and not
subject to each other's limited perspectives (14:4, 10-12); and (3)
since participation in the kingdom of God is not determined by
what we eat or drink, neither abstaining nor partaking is a cause
for judgmentalism (14:13, 17).

Having shown that both the strong and the weak are to be
faulted for their attitude toward each other (14:10), Paul nonetheless surfaces a special concern for the weak ones (14:15-16).
In this he is clearly in keeping with the special divine concern for
"the weak ones" throughout the Old and New Testaments. A
strong faith is less vulnerable than a weak faith. In the race of
faith toward the finish line (see Phil 3:13-14), the strong are less
likely to stumble over some obstacle than the weak. Therefore,
the eating of foods which the weak believe to be unclean is an
act which is potentially dangerous for those of young faith
(14:13-14). It is an unloving act by the strong if a fellow Christian
"is distressed because of what you eat" (v. 15). In light of the rest
of the verse ("Do not by your eating destroy your brother for
whom Christ died") the NIV rendering "distressed" is probably
too mild. The Greek word *lypeō*, in addition to "grieve," "pain,"
"distress," can also mean "to injure," "damage" (as in RSV). In-
juring another's faith may lead to its ultimate destruction.

As in 1 Corinthians, so here, Paul is deeply concerned about
Christians growth toward mature faith and their eternal well-
being. The imperative of love (verse 15) means that Christians
are to act in ways which build each other up rather than in ways
which tear each other down (vv. 19-20), in ways which hold each
other up and help each other along rather than in ways which

cause others "to stumble" and "to fall" (vv. 20-21).

The basis for this kind of Christian conduct is the principle: "Each of us should please his neighbor for his good, to build him up," which Paul articulates at the conclusion of the discussion (15:2) and grounds in the life of Jesus: "For even Christ did not please himself" (15:3). In the final analysis Christian conduct is grounded in Christ's self-giving, sacrificial love (15:8).

Paul does not tell us how to discern, specifically, when our conduct will bring injury to a fellow believer's spiritual life and possibly to a falling into sin's sphere of domination. What he does seem to believe deeply is that when life is lived in fellowship with Christ, driven by his love, seeking to imitate his life, then we will have the kind of sensitivity to each other which will prevent us from harmful acts.

• C H A P T E R 1 4 •

Destroying God's Temple

If anyone destroys God's temple,
God will destroy him;
for God's temple is sacred,
and you are that temple.
1 CORINTHIANS 3:17

The difficulty of this passage has to do both with the meaning of the important terms used and with the implications of it for our living as Christians. Who, or what, is God's temple? By what actions or lifestyle or words can this "temple of God" be destroyed? Are the words or deeds which destroy this temple of God like the "unforgivable sin" which cannot be forgiven (Mt 12:22-32), since they bring down the judgment of God ("God will destroy him")?

A careful study of the grammar and structure of the passage, as well as its place in Paul's overall argument in the opening chapter of this letter, will help us in getting at these questions.

The most pervasive and common understanding of our text holds that Paul is here talking about our individual bodies as temples or dwellings of God's Spirit (3:16). If we destroy these "temples"—through the way we live (for example, through sexual impurity) or by what we put into our bodies (for example, alcohol, drugs, tobacco, gluttony) or by what we do to them (for example, suicide)—we become the objects of God's final, destructive judgment. For, since our bodies are both created by God and the objects of God's redemptive work, they are sacred and should not be destroyed in these ways by us.

These are all important and true biblical insights, and Paul specifically addresses the issue of the proper use of our physical bodies with regard to sexuality later in this epistle (chapter 6). But Paul is not speaking to these important issues in this text. Our physical, individual bodies are not what he is here concerned about. Both for grammatical and contextual reasons, these popular understandings must be set aside in order to truly hear God's word for the Corinthians and for us in this text.

Let's look at the grammatical matter first. First Corinthians 3:16-17 forms one unit of thought and must be treated as such. This is recognized by most English translations, which set verses 16-17 apart in a distinct paragraph, and is clear from the fact that both verses speak of God's temple.

The question "Who or what is God's temple?" is answered when we understand Paul's use of the personal pronoun "you" in verses 16-17. For readers of the English text, the verbs "you know," "you are" and the pronoun "you" can be either singular (a particular individual) or plural (a group of persons). Reading the text with the singular "you" in mind has led to the popular confusion discussed above. However, in the Greek language, there are different words for singular "you" and plural "you" (that is, "you all"). Further, verbs have distinct endings which show whether the subject of the verb is singular or plural, first person ("I," "we"), second person ("you," "you all") or third person ("he," "she," "it" or "they"). Thus, the Greek text of verses 16-17 is unambiguous regarding the number of the "you" addressed; the verb endings and pronouns all reflect the plural "you."

Among modern translations, only the NIV and TEV make a partial attempt at accurately rendering the Greek. In verse 16 the NIV reads, "Do you not know that you yourselves are God's temple?" In verse 17 the TEV reads, "and you yourselves are that temple." Yet, even these do not bring out the meaning as clearly as the Greek. The following annotated rendering is an attempt to catch the precision of the Greek: "Do you (the many) not know that you (the many) are God's temple and that God's Spirit lives in (among) you (the many)? Anyone who destroys God's temple will be destroyed by God; for God's temple is sacred, and you (the many) are that temple."

This recognition of the nuances of Paul's Greek shows that he is not here thinking of individual Christians as temples inhabited by God, but of the church, the fellowship of believers in Corinth, among whom the Spirit of God dwells and is operative. Paul expresses this same sense in 2 Corinthians 6:16 where he says that "we are the temple of the living God." If he had wished to address individual Christians in their physical bodies, Paul would have had to say in 3:16, "Don't you know that you are temples of God?" and in 3:17, "You are those temples." (And in 2 Corinthians 6:16, "We are the temples of the living God".)

In many ways, 3:16-17 reveals Paul's foundational understanding of the church and is a key to the meaning of the entire letter. Namely, the church, the people of God among whom God's Spirit dwells, is God's option, God's alternative to the fragmentation and brokenness of human society. The Christian congregation gathered in Corinth was called to model that alternative in the midst of the brokenness of Corinthian society. But their divisive-

ness, their immorality, their enthusiastic spirituality which dis-
regarded concrete, bodily dimensions of life—all these were destroying the viability of God's option, God's temple, in Corinth.
And it is that destruction which stands under God's judgment.

This corporate understanding of God's temple in verses 16-17
is confirmed by the context. Paul is occupied in the first four
chapters of this epistle with divisions which are threatening the
very life of the church (1:10-17; 3:3-4). These schisms apparently
centered around loyalty to certain teachings which the Corinthian Christians had received from either their founder (Paul) or
from leaders who worked among them after Paul's departure
(Apollos, Peter—1:12).

In this section (3:10-15), Paul shows that those called to leadership in the church, and perhaps all Christians, are accountable
to God for the way in which they participate, through life and
work, in the growth of God's building. It is possible to build with
materials that endure (gold, silver) or with materials that are of
inferior quality (hay, stubble—3:12). The end-time judgment
("the day"—3:13), pictured here as elsewhere in Scripture as a
fiery ordeal, will reveal with what materials individuals have
built (3:13-15). It may be, as some commentators have suggested,
that Paul has the followers of Peter and Apollos in mind. The
former may be attempting to build their own legalistic Jewish
practices into the structure of the church; the latter may be
building with eloquent (worldly) wisdom and superspirituality.
These "building materials," as Paul shows throughout his writings (particularly Gal and 1 Cor) are ultimately useless. Though
Christians who build with these materials are not excluded from
God's salvation, their passage through God's judgment into eternity will be accompanied by the experience of failure and loss
(3:15).

But beyond the danger of using worthless building materials
in the growth of God's people, there is the greater danger of

acting and living in such a way that "God's building" will in fact
be destroyed. It is that danger which Paul addresses in 3:17.

The congregation of people composing the church at Corinth
was in danger of destroying itself. As the entire catalog of problems with which Paul deals in this epistle reveals, the possibility
of this church's destruction was real: their haughtiness regarding
the presence of flagrant immorality (chapter 5); their use of pagan courts for settling internal disputes and the continuing participation of certain members in pagan rites of cultic prostitution
(chapter 6); the use of Christian freedom and knowledge in such
a way that the "weak in faith" would fall back into sin and be
destroyed (chapters 8, 10); the rejection of Paul's teaching on the
resurrection of the body in favor of an emphasis on purely "spiritual redemption" (chapter 15), which led the Corinthians to a
total disregard for the concrete, practical dimensions of life within the fellowship and the larger society.

To destroy the church, this temple of God, is to destroy God's
alternative to the brokenness of human society; it is to make it
impossible for God's redemptive presence and work, through his
"temple" in Corinth, to redeem Corinthian society. Those who
thus oppose the very redemptive purposes of God—by factious
and contentious, acrimonious behavior; by false doctrines which
reject the message of the cross as scandalous and foolish; by
perverting the freedom of the gospel into unrestrained libertinism; by replacing salvation by grace through faith with legalistic
dependence on works—are liable to God's destroying power.
Their destruction, however, is not to be seen as an act of vindictive retribution, but rather as the inevitable result that comes
to those who reject God's way of salvation.

It is in this sense that the one who "destroys the temple of
God" belongs to the category of those who, according to Jesus
in Matthew 12:22-32, commit the unpardonable sin. There, it is
the rejection of the redemptive presence of God's Spirit in the life

and ministry of Jesus. To reject that work of God is to refuse God's forgiveness. For Paul, it is the destruction of God's way of salvation through the church, in which the Spirit of God is operative (3:16) that leads to destruction. For to destroy this work of God (see Rom 14:20) is, in the final analysis, the rejection of God.

• C H A P T E R 1 5 •

Handing
Over to
Satan

Hand this man over to Satan,
so that the sinful nature may be destroyed
and his spirit saved on the
day of the Lord.
1 CORINTHIANS 5:5

This instruction of Paul to the Christians in Corinth, which is part of his call for the excommunication of a member because of serious immorality, needs careful interpretation, or else considerable distortion of his meaning is possible.

Questions such as the following are often asked: What does "handing over to Satan" really mean? Why would the apostle want anyone to be handed over to Satan? Though the man committed a grievous sin, is there no room for discipline and forgiveness within the Christian community? What is envisioned in the term "destruction of his sinful nature" (literally "flesh")? And how can that possibly be a means toward "salvation of his spirit"?

Let us follow Paul's argument and seek to understand the terms used by him in the larger context of his thought.

In our interpretation of 1 Corinthians 3:17 (chapter 14 above) we held that Paul understood the church, in its local manifestation in Corinth (and any other place) to be God's alternative to the fragmentation and brokenness of human society. The viability of that alternative was being undermined in a number of ways in the church at Corinth. Chapter 5, where our hard saying is located, deals in its entirety with one of these ways.

The specific problem is the sexually immoral life being led by one of the members. The larger problem is an attitude about physical life among the Corinthian Christians which allows them not merely to be tolerant of the immoral behavior of a brother, but to exhibit a certain pride, yea arrogance, about the matter. We shall address these in order.

Paul lays the matter clearly before them in 5:1. The word rendered "sexual immorality" (NIV), or simply "immorality" (RSV), is the Greek word *porneia* (from which we derive "pornography"). Literally, it means "prostitution," but Paul uses it, as normally throughout the New Testament, in its broader meaning of sexual impurity of various kinds. The following sentence, "A man has his father's wife," points out the nature of the immorality. The verb *has* is in the present infinitive form, indicating that the situation is not a single occurrence, but a continuing immoral affair. It is not defined as incest, so the woman is likely his stepmother. Nor does Paul speak of adultery; thus, her husband is either dead or she is divorced from him.

Alone from Paul's Jewish perspective, such a relationship is a serious break of divine law. Leviticus 18:8 clearly forbids it, and according to rabbinic tradition, the offender was liable to stoning. What makes the situation even more grave is the recognition, stated in 5:1, that such a sexual relationship is "of a kind that does not occur even among pagans." By this Paul is probably not claiming that this kind of immorality never occurs among pagans; rather, he must be referring to the fact that even Roman law (as stated in the Institutes of Gaius) forbade such a practice (that is, "Even in the pagan world this is unheard of as acceptable behavior!"). It was clearly detrimental to the moral fiber of the entire congregation, as well as the viability of its witness in the pagan world.

The seriousness of this matter, which elicits Paul's rather harsh judgment and direction for congregational action, is undergirded by his assessment of the congregation's attitude, which apparently not only tolerated this illicit union, but found in it an occasion of prideful boasting. Indeed, Paul may have seen, behind their attitude, a view of Christian faith and life which promoted and nurtured the kind of sexual immorality addressed (both here in chapter 5, as well as another form of it in chapter 6).

"The man is having sexual relations with his father's wife—intolerable in both Jewish religious and Roman civil law—and you are proud" (5:2). This judgment on their attitude is anticipated already in chapter 4. Here, Paul throws a series of sarcastic barbs at their lofty pride: "already you have become rich!", "you have become kings" (4:8); "you are so wise in Christ!", "you are strong!" (4:10). Then he sums it up with the words "Some of you have become arrogant" (4:18). After his instruction about the excommunication of the offender, he points again to their attitude: "your boasting is not good" (5:6).

What is the ground for this lofty arrogance? It has long been recognized that many of the problems which Paul addresses in the church at Corinth seem to be grounded in a religious mindset which devalued physical life and emphasized spiritual liberation. This view developed out of Hellenistic syncretism, with contributions from both philosophy and mystical cults that spread across the Roman empire from the Orient.

Plato had taught that the body was the tomb of the soul; that death brought liberation from physical captivity; that already in this life one could transcend the negative arena of matter by a higher knowledge of ultimate reality. Various Hellenistic cults offered immortality via union with the god or gods, sometimes symbolized or achieved through cultic prostitution. Within such a religious philosophical climate, Paul's teaching regarding freedom "in Christ" and life "in the Spirit" was all too often, and particularly at Corinth, perverted into an enthusiastic libertinism which rejected moral restraints, particularly in the realm of the physical. Since the physical realm is by definition of no account—so they seem to have argued—it does not really matter what we do with our bodies. Indeed, their arrogant pride regarding sexual immorality in their midst indicates that they may have seen this matter as the very proof of their spiritual perfection. Theirs was a religion of enthusiastic intoxication without moral enthusiasm!

The proper response, both to the intolerable case of sexual immorality, as well as to their imagined superior spirituality, should have been mourning, not pride (5:2). And such an attitude would inevitably lead to the removal of the offender from the fellowship.

That some form of excommunication is intended is clear, not only from 5:2, but from the Passover analogy in 5:6-8 ("Get rid of the old yeast" —5:7) and the citation of Deuteronomy 17:7 ("Expel the wicked man from among you"—5:13). The nature of the removal is expressed in the ambiguous phrase "hand this man over to Satan." Its purpose is twofold: (1) that his "flesh" would be destroyed and (2) that his "spirit" would be saved (5:5).

The phrase "hand over to Satan" must be recognized in some figurative, metaphorical sense, since a person literally abandoned to Satan would seem to be lost irrevocably. Yet here such an end is not envisioned.

Some have seen behind the expression the Jewish practice of excommunication, imposed particularly for infringement against

marriage laws. In banning an offender, it was believed that separation from the people of God, and therefore from God's special
care, would lead to premature death. (Yet, within Jewish practice,
the hand of God was understood to execute this punishment, not
Satan). Premature death, in this view, could be referred to by
"destruction of the flesh." How this premature death would af-
fect a final salvation is not clear.

It seems best to find an explanation within the larger background of apocalyptic Jewish thought which Paul shared. According to that thought, Satan was understood as the "ruler of
this world" (see Jn 12:31), as the "prince of darkness" with sovereignty over "this present evil age" and the realm of death.
According to the Gospels, Jesus' teachings and deeds are the
reign of God breaking into the realm of Satan's dominion (see Lk
11:14-22). For Paul, Jesus' death and resurrection were the decisive events: the evil powers had been robbed of their control
(Col 2:15); the "end of the ages" had broken into this present evil
age (1 Cor 10:11); the "new creation" had dawned (2 Cor 5:17);
Christians were people who had been delivered "from the dominion of darkness" and transferred into the kingdom of God's beloved Son (Col 1:13).

Within this larger understanding of Paul's view the expression
"hand him over to Satan" must be interpreted. The new creation
had begun, but had not yet been consummated; the dominion of
evil had been invaded, but had not yet ended; the new age had
superimposed itself on this present evil age, but had not yet
replaced it. Thus the church was the arena of Christ's presence
and continuing work; it was the community of God's Spirit. To
be excommunicated was therefore to be transferred out of the
kingdom of God's Son into the dominion of darkness (a reversal
of Col 1:13!). Such a transaction is aptly described as a "handing
over to Satan," that is, into the world, the sphere of his continuing domain.

If that is the proper sense of the phrase, then how are we to understand the stated purposes of this transaction?

A literal reading of the phrase, "for the destruction of the flesh," leads to several possible meanings: (1) abandonment of the man's physical existence to the powers of destruction; (2) premature death, in keeping with Jewish ideas; (3) physical sufferings. Two difficulties arise: (1) How do any of these lead to the stated purpose of the excommunication—namely, salvation? (2) In light of Paul's teaching regarding bodily resurrection and his rejection of Corinthian libertinism (with its antiphysical thrust), would he be promoting the dichotomy: destruction of the flesh versus salvation of the spirit?

These difficulties disappear when we take seriously the way in which Paul uses the terms *flesh* and *spirit* generally when speaking about human life. Paul clearly rejected the dichotomy between the physical and the spiritual so prevalent in Greek thought. When he contrasts "flesh" with "spirit" in human existence, being "in the flesh" with being "in the spirit," he is contrasting two means of existence, two orientations of life. "Flesh" represents the total being (including the human spirit) in its opposition to God; "spirit" designates the total being (including the physical) as redeemed by God, in relation with Christ. (For a fuller discussion, see chapter five on Rom 7:14, 19.)

The NIV rendering of the literal Greek—"for destruction of the flesh"—with "so that the sinful nature may be destroyed" rightly catches Paul's "religious" use of the word *flesh*. The aim of the excommunication would then have been the destruction of the offender's "way of life." Surely he had grasped something of God's grace, experienced dimensions of Christ's love in the fellowship, witnessed the Spirit's transforming power in the lives of his brothers and sisters. Excluded from this sphere, might he not come to his senses (like the Prodigal Son)? Might he not come to the recognition that his immorality would only lead to death, but that the death of his immorality would lead to life?

Only in such an understanding is the concept "destruction of the flesh" an appropriate preliminary step to "salvation of his spirit." In this last phrase, "spirit" denotes the human being as regenerated by the Spirit of God, living "in the Spirit" or "according to the Spirit" (see Rom 8:5-11). As such, the one who had once again been claimed from the dominion of darkness, through the destruction of his "fleshly" orientation, would be saved "on the day of the Lord."

• C H A P T E R 1 6 •

Who
Inherits the
Kingdom?

*Do not be deceived: Neither the sexually immoral
nor idolaters nor adulterers nor male prostitutes
nor homosexual offenders nor thieves nor the greedy
nor drunkards nor slanderers nor swindlers
will inherit the kingdom of God.*
1 CORINTHIANS 6:9-10

After reading 1 Corinthians 6:9-10, some persons breathe a sigh
of relief. They see that they are not included in this list of vices
which disqualify persons from membership in the kingdom of
God. Others read this list and even though they are not guilty
of the major sexual sins and criminal activities listed, they recognize that they are sometimes dishonest, or want more things
than they need, or have said things which hurt other people, or
have an alcoholic problem. Are they excluded from the kingdom?
Still others reading this text who have misused the gift of sexual
intimacy outside the boundaries of the covenant of marriage, or
who find themselves overpowered by a homosexual orientation

and its expression, hear in this text a harsh word of judgment and condemnation.

The question "Who inherits the kingdom?" becomes even more acute when we recognize that the list of sins enumerated here is only representative and not exhaustive. Paul catalogs several other vices that exclude people from kingdom membership. In Galatians 5:19-21, in addition to sexual immorality, idolatry and drunkenness (which are in the 1 Cor text), Paul lists the following: impurity, debauchery, witchcraft, hatred, discord, jealousy, fits of rage, selfish ambition, dissensions, factions, envy, orgies. He closes the list with these words: "Those who live like this will not inherit the kingdom of God."

The lists in Ephesians 5:3-5 and Colossians 3:5-9 share some of those already in the other two and add a few more: obscenity, foolish talk, coarse joking, evil desire, anger, malice, lying. The Ephesians list also speaks of disqualification from kingdom membership (5:5). In Colossians, Paul assigns these sins to the "earthly nature" (3:5), the "old self" (3:10), "the life you once lived" (3:7), and tells them they must rid themselves of these (3:8), for they have no place in the "new self" (3:10) which "will appear with [Christ] in glory" (3:4).

Once we have read all of Paul's lists, we become painfully aware that even those among us who breathed a sigh of relief after reading 1 Corinthians 6:9-10 are also tainted and, as such, disqualified from kingdom membership. And so we are tempted to ask, with Jesus' disciples, "Who then can be saved?" (Lk 18:26). We shall see that Paul's answer to this question is surely the same as Jesus' response to his disciples: "What is impossible with men is possible with God" (Lk 18:27).

In 1 Corinthians 5, Paul has addressed the presence of a particularly scandalous case of sexual immorality (see chapter 15, above). After calling for action which could lead to the offenders' salvation, Paul speaks about the nature of the Christian fellowship via elements from the Jewish Passover (5:6-8). The church is like the dough used for the Passover bread. Yeast, which in the Old Testament symbolizes evil, is to be removed so the dough can become uncontaminated, unleavened bread. So in the church a little yeast (for example, sexual immorality, a haughty spirit) contaminates the whole batch of dough (the church, 5:6). The church must remove the yeast so it can be a new batch without yeast, which, in a real sense, it already is (5:7).

We have here a typical example of Paul's understanding of both the church and individual believers as living in the tension between the "already" and the "not yet." The church is the present expression of the reign of God, the kingdom of God in the midst of the world; but it is still on the way, not yet identical with the kingdom of God at the end of history. Christians have been set free from the bondage to sin; yet they must appropriate that freedom in specific decisions to resist the encroachments of evil continually (see Rom 6).

In 1 Corinthians 6 (where our hard saying is located), Paul exposes another fragment of "yeast" which needs to be dealt with. The spectacle of church members taking each other to civil court underlines the "not yet" dimension of the church. They cheat and wrong each other (6:8)!

These evidences of unrighteousness among the Corinthian believers lead Paul to denounce all forms of evil as incompatible with the kingdom of God: "Do you not know that the wicked will not inherit the kingdom of God?" (6:9). Why? Because by definition, the future kingdom of God is one of absolute righteousness, since the forces of evil have been overcome (see 1 Cor 15:24-28). In such a kingdom, the unrighteous will have no part.

As we saw in the discussion of 1 Corinthians 5:5 (chapter 15), not only was Paul concerned about specific acts of immorality or conduct incompatible with our status as the community of the Spirit. He was also concerned with a religious view which disre-

garded practical morality and thus encouraged, perhaps even affirmed, immoral and unethical behavior. Toward that stance,
Paul is emphatic: "Do not be deceived." (6:9). The Corinthians
were deluding themselves into believing that God's moral demands did not need to be taken seriously. But to reject God's
moral imperatives is to reject membership in God's kingdom (6:9-
10).

Having laid the cards on the table so there could be no misunderstanding about the lofty goal of Christian life and faith
(that is, a kingdom of perfect righteousness), Paul now reminds
them of God's transforming intervention in their former lives of
unrighteousness. "That is what some of you were" (6:11). Paul
had founded the church several years earlier (4:15), and the faces
of his converts, including the lives they had lived, may have
flashed across his mind as he was penning the list of representative vices which are incompatible with God's kingdom. "But
you were washed, you were sanctified, you were justified in the
name of the Lord Jesus Christ and by the Spirit of our God"
(6:11).

Paul reminds them of what is possible when the broken and
sin-scarred wrecks of human lives are yielded to God in faith and
touched by his grace. They were the result of a miracle, redeemed sinners won from destructive ways of life by God's power. The image of having been "washed" surely recalled their baptism and reminded them of what the ritual symbolized: an
inward cleansing brought about by God's forgiving love in
Christ. Further, they were "sanctified." In this context the term
does not have the more technical meaning, namely, that of
moral-ethical growth toward perfection. Rather, it reminds them
that through baptism they became part of the people of God,
whom Paul called "saints." Finally, they are reminded that they
were justified, called back into right relationship with God, on
the basis of God's relation-restoring love in Christ.

On the ground of this action of God and their faith response in the past, Paul can speak of them in analogy to the Passover dough as really unleavened, free from evil. Yet, on the basis of their present reality, marred by acts and lifestyles of unrighteousness, he can call them to become what they are, to remove from their fellowship and their individual lives "the yeast of malice and wickedness" (5:8), to "flee from sexual immorality" (6:18), to honor God with their bodies (6:20). How is that possible? It is possible because their bodies are the dwelling places of the Spirit of God (6:19), who can continue to transform them toward conformity with the image of their creator (see also Col 3:10).

Who inherits the kingdom? All those whose lives have been scarred by one or more of the sins in the Pauline lists with which we began, whose scarred lives have been healed and cleansed by the grace of God, and who reject the continuing encroachments of sin, moving in the power of the Spirit toward the coming kingdom of the Lord.

Paul's words to the Christians in Ephesus, in the context of one of his catalog of vices, are an apt summary for this chapter: "For you were once darkness, but now you are light in the Lord. Live as children of light. . . . Have nothing to do with the fruitless deeds of darkness" (Eph 5:8, 11).

· C H A P T E R   1 7 ·

Is It
Good to
Marry?

*It is good for a man
not to marry.*
1 CORINTHIANS 7:1

P aul's statement that *"it is good for a man not to marry,"* at the beginning of a chapter in which he deals with issues of singleness, celibacy and marriage, as well as the appropriate place for the expression of sexuality, has raised numerous questions. This is so especially for those who take the Bible seriously as the ultimate authority for Christian life and faith.

If Paul is teaching that singleness and celibacy are superior expressions of Christian spirituality, then are all Christians who are married and choose to marry opting for an inferior lifestyle? How are Christian young people, in the process of making vocational and relational decisions about their future, to respond to

Paul's words? Are they deciding against "the best" God has for them and for "the lesser good," namely, their physical-psychological needs, the passions of their flesh, if they decide to marry?

Yes would seem to be the obvious answer in light of both this text and others such as in 7:7 ("I wish that all were as I am"), 7:8 ("It is good for [the unmarried and widows] to stay unmarried, as I am") and 7:26 ("it is good for [virgins] to remain as you are").

Even if we are not to take Paul's apparent preference for celibacy as an expression of God's optimum will, the value and expression of physical, sexual intimacy seems to be viewed somewhat negatively, in light of statements such as 7:2 ("But since there is so much immorality, each man should have his own wife"), 7:5 ("come together again so that Satan will not tempt you because of your lack of self-control") and 7:9 ("But if [the unmarried] cannot control themselves, they should marry").

If we are to deal fairly with our "hard saying" and the way in which Paul explores its implications in the rest of chapter 7, we need to take seriously some of the principles for the interpretation of the epistles which we discussed in the introduction to this book. One of these is the recognition that the epistles (and 1 Cor more so than perhaps any of the others) are occasional documents, written for specific situations in the life of Christian congregations. Thus, in the case of 1 Corinthians, Paul is responding to concerns and problems (in chapters 1-4) which have been communicated to him orally, apparently by a church delegation (1:11). In chapter 7 he begins his response to matters which had been laid before him in a letter: "Now for the matters you wrote about" (7:1; see also 8:1; 12:1; 16:1). Though Paul does not explicitly tell us what they wrote, we have a good general idea about what the issues were for which they sought his advice or counsel.

A second principle of importance is the recognition of the particular historical or cultural or church context within which the needs or questions addressed by the apostle are located. Thus the pervasive sexual immorality in Corinthian society, which even spilled over into the church (Paul deals with it in 1 Corinthians 5—6; see chapters 15 and 16 above), needs to be kept in mind when we read 7:1-24. Also to be remembered is the Corinthian Christians' view regarding the dichotomy between the spiritual and the physical, which led to various responses regarding human sexuality. In chapter 15 we discussed the nature of this perspective and how it resulted in a libertine view of sex ("anything goes!"). In 1 Corinthians 7, Paul seems to be responding to the "ascetic" implications of their negative views regarding the physical.

A third principle of significance for understanding the saying in 7:1 (as well as many other sayings dealt with in the following chapters of this book) is to recognize that the inspired, authoritative word of the apostle may be either *normative* for Christian life and faith generally, transcending all times and situations, or it may be *corrective*, intended to address a particular issue in a particular context, without necessarily intending to have universal application.

With these perspectives in mind, the issues Paul raises for us in 7:1 and several other "hard sayings" in 7:10, 12, 20 and 29 (see chapters 18-20 below) can be more easily understood.

The Greek sentence translated "It is good for a man not to marry" in NIV and TEV (7:1) is more literally translated "It is well for a man not to touch a woman" in NASB and RSV. The NIV gives this alternative reading in a footnote: "It is good for a man not to have sexual relations with a woman." That rendering recognizes that the term "to touch" is a biblical euphemism for sexual intimacy (see Gen 20:6, Prov 6:29). Since for Paul sexual intimacy and the covenant of marriage clearly belong together, the term "to touch a woman" can legitimately refer to marrying. The verses which follow 7:1 strongly support such a meaning.

On the basis of the introductory phrase, "Now for the matters you wrote about," and several other places in the letter where Paul seems to be quoting slogans which the Corinthians waved in his face in support of their position (see 6:12-13 and 10:23), several modern translations suggest an alternative reading for 7:1: "You say that a man does well not to marry" (TEV; see also the footnote rendering in the NEB, "You say, 'It is a good thing for a man to have nothing to do with a woman.' "). Attributing our hard saying to the Corinthian position might lessen the problems raised at the outset, except for the fact that, if it is their slogan, Paul seems to cite it with at least restrained approval and certainly personalizes the sentiment expressed later in the same chapter (7:7, 8, 26).

What the slogan—whether a citation from the Corinthians' letter to Paul or Paul's summary of their views—clearly reveals is an attitude about marriage and sexual expression within it that advocates asceticism. The lofty (and haughty) spirituality of some believers in Corinth expressed itself—in relation to concrete, physical things—in the attitude, "everything is permissible" (6:12). That same spirituality could also express itself in an ascetic attitude, the rejection of all physical, sensual aspects of life. That is apparently the view with which Paul does battle in most of chapter 7. Not only did some reject marriage, as such, as unworthy of "true spirituality," some even rejected the expression of sexual desire within marriage. And for still others, divorce seemed to be desirable as a means for developing their spirituality apart from the sexual intimacy of marriage.

Within this larger context then, Paul's personal preference for celibacy, and his equally strong affirmation of the goodness of marriage and of sexual intimacy within it, needs to be understood.

The affirmation "It is good for a man *not* to marry" does not necessarily or logically lead to the conclusion "It is *not* good for a man to marry." Paul affirms the value of singleness and the celibate state, but he does not devalue marriage and sex within it. This is shown in what follows, where he strongly qualifies the statement "it is good not to marry" and lifts up the purposes of marriage.

In 7:2-7, he affirms one of these good purposes: "Since there is so much immorality," normally people should marry. This conviction is grounded in Paul's view of created design and order, according to Genesis 1—2. God created the human species as male and female (Gen 1:26-27), with and for each other, in complementary polarity. Aloneness "is not good"; God creates the woman "corresponding to him" (Gen 2:18). Therefore the man and the woman are united in the covenant of marriage and become "one flesh" (Gen 2:24).

Paul recognizes this divinely created and ordained context for human intimacy and the expression of the sexual drive. In light of the pervasive sexual immorality (that is, sex outside the male-female covenant of marriage) in Corinth and even in the church (1 Cor 5—6), Paul affirms that one of the purposes of marriage is the legitimate expression of the God-given drive toward physical union. Sex in marriage is not to be rejected. Setting it aside should only be by mutual decision and for a limited period of time (7:5), not (by implication) because it is of no value or hurtful. God-given sexuality is a strong force. If it is not given its proper context for expression, it is in danger of spilling over into sexual immorality (7:5).

For Paul, the temporary setting aside of sexual intimacy in marriage is "a concession, not a command" (7:6). The norm in marriage is the mutual right of the partners to each other in physical union. The concession (a limited time of abstinence for the purpose of prayer—7:5) seems to be for the sake of the Corinthian ascetics, who probably wanted to abstain totally.

Paul concludes this carefully balanced discussion by affirming

CHAPTER 18

Not I, but the Lord

To the married I give this command
(not I, but the Lord): . . .
To the rest I say this
(I, not the Lord).
1 CORINTHIANS 7:10, 12

The distinction which Paul makes here between a command which has its origin in the Lord and instruction which he gives to the church has raised questions for many readers. If, in terms of authority, there is no proper distinction between a word from the Lord and Paul's opinion, why does Paul seem to distinguish so clearly between what the Lord commands and what he himself has to say? If Paul intends to make a distinction between levels of authority, what are the implications of that distinction for the authority of the Gospels relative to Paul's letters? Do we need to scrutinize all of Paul's writings in light of Jesus' teaching in the Gospels and elevate those parts of his letters which are that his own celibacy, which he has experienced as a great good and therefore wished for others also, is a gift from God (7:7). This gift provides singleness of purpose in the service of Christ (7:8-9, 32-35). Those who are not gifted in this way have other gifts which they should exercise.

The latter part of the chapter (7:25-35) makes clear that Paul's preference for celibacy and his wish that others follow his example is strongly grounded in the early church's expectation that the reign of God—which had broken into this present age in Jesus' life, death and resurrection—would soon be consummated, perhaps even in their lifetime (7:26, "because of the present crisis"; 7:29, "the time is short"; 7:31, "this world in its present form is passing away"). In light of this brevity of time, Paul is concerned that Christians who have the opportunity—because they are not yet, or no longer, married—be involved in the work of the Lord, spreading the good news (7:32, 35). This eschatological urgency helps to explain Paul's passionate commitment regarding the value of celibacy, while at the same time strongly arguing against the Corinthian ascetics in behalf of marriage and the expression of God-intended sexual intimacy within it.

clearly corroborated by Jesus' teaching above those which are clearly the product of Paul's thought?

Beyond these questions regarding the authority of what Paul wrote is the more basic issue of Paul's apostolic authority. In several documents from his hand (including the Corinthian correspondence), his apostolic authority is a key concern. His sometimes harsh words to the schismatics at Corinth, as well as to the hyperspiritualists (1 Cor) and his opponents (2 Cor), seem to be grounded in a clear sense of apostolic authority, which he asserts and defends vigorously. What then does he mean to communicate by saying, "I say this (I, not the Lord)"?

Paul's understanding of his apostolic authority must be seen against the background of his Jewish heritage and in light of his experience of the risen Lord and his sense of divinely ordained vocation.

Within Judaism, rabbinic authority was grounded in the God-given Torah. Those learned in the law received, interpreted and passed on the authoritative tradition because they sat "in Moses' seat" (Mt 23:2). Their authority as teachers of the law was a derived authority, but it was nonetheless binding because it was understood to be in continuity with the primary authority.

Just as Paul once was a student of the rabbis and was "extremely zealous for the traditions" of his fathers (Gal 1:14)—who derived their authority from Moses, and therefore from the God who gave his law to Moses—so he now could pronounce a curse on anyone who preached any gospel other than the one he preached and the Galatians had accepted (Gal 1:8-9). Why? Because the gospel which he preached was not of human origin; rather it had its origin in the Lord (Gal 1:11-12). Thus not only Paul's gospel, but the teaching derived from it, is rooted in the authority of Christ. Therefore Paul's instruction to churches and individuals is to be received, not as merely human words, but as the word of God (1 Thess 2:13).

Further, Paul stands within the chain of "receiving" and "passing on" the authoritative tradition (see 1 Cor 11:2, 23; 15:1-3). He knows that he has been grasped by Christ (Phil 3:12), that he is a recipient of Christ's authoritative revelation (1 Cor 15:9-11) and that he is called to be an apostle not through human instrumentality, but by direct divine intervention (Gal 1:1). Though it is doubtful that the word *apostolos* had in this early period the later technical sense of "office" (occupied by the Twelve plus Paul), its primary meaning, "one sent," certainly involved for Paul the authority of the Sender (see Rom 1:1; 1 Cor 1:1).

As one endowed with the authority of the Sender, his message and preaching are a demonstration of the power of God's Spirit (1 Cor 2:4). As God's Sent One *(apostolos)*, his instruction to excommunicate an offender is accompanied by "the power of our Lord Jesus" (1 Cor 5:4).

In light of his self-understanding of apostolic authority, it is very improbable that Paul's words in 1 Corinthians 7:10 and 12 indicate a lessening of that sense of authority.

Throughout chapter 7, Paul frequently adopts a pastoral role, giving advice and counsel. He expresses the wish that others were as he is (v. 7). He lays options before them and calls on them to make responsible choices (vv. 8-9, 28, 36-38). He gives instruction for a course of action in light of his concern for them (vv. 32-35). When Paul speaks in this mode, it is quite clear that he is not demanding obedience; yet he makes it also quite clear that he does not simply express neutral human opinion. His opinion does have behind it "the Spirit of God" (v. 40), and he does want them to know that he is trustworthy as one guided by the Lord's mercy (v. 25).

However, the instruction which follows the words "I say this (I, not the Lord)" is surely an application—in a new situation—of the instruction which follows the words "I give this command (not I, but the Lord)." The distinction Paul makes is simply this: In the matter of divorce and remarriage, Paul is in possession of a direct command of the Lord. It can hardly be doubted that his instruction in 7:10-11 is based on the teaching of Jesus preserved for us in Mark 10:2-12. But for the question of what is to be done when a believer is married to a nonbeliever, Paul was not in possession of a direct teaching from Jesus. Jesus did not address this issue during his ministry. Thus, after appealing to the direct teaching of Jesus regarding the sanctity and permanence of marriage as intended by the Creator, Paul goes on, after simply acknowledging that he does not have another direct word from the Lord, to apply the implications of that divine intention to the complex situation of marriages between believers and unbelievers. The thrust of the passage makes it difficult, if not impossible, to assume that Paul intended his words to convey a lessened sense of authority.

CHAPTER 19

Remain Where You Are

*Each one should remain
in the situation which he was
in when God called him.*
1 CORINTHIANS 7:20

The difficulty with which *1 Corinthians 7:20 presents us arises pri*marily from the surrounding verses in the paragraph (vv. 17-24). In verse 21 the situation chosen as an illustration is that of slavery. In verse 17 the various situations in which persons found themselves when they were called to faith in Christ are understood as assigned or apportioned by the Lord, and they are told to remain in those situations. That instruction is given further weight in the sentence, "This is the rule I lay down in all the churches" (v. 17).

In light of these statements, Paul has often been charged, not only with failure to condemn the evil system of slavery, but indeed with abetting the status quo. These charges can be demonstrated to be invalid when the paragraph which contains our text is seen within the total context of chapter 7 and in light of the historical situation as Paul perceived it.

In chapter 7 Paul is dealing with questions about marriage, the appropriate place for sexual expression, the issue of divorce and remarriage, all in response to a pervasive view in the church which rejected or demeaned the physical dimension of male-female relationships (see chapter 17 above). In the immediately preceding paragraph (7:12-16), Paul's counsel to believers who are married to unbelievers is twofold: (1) If the unbelieving partner is willing to remain in the marriage, the believer should not divorce (and thus reject) the unbelieving partner. For that person's willingness to live with the believer may open him or her to the sanctifying power of God's grace through the believing partner (7:12-14); (2) if the unbeliever does not want to remain in the union, he or she should be released from the marriage. Though the partner may be sanctified through the life and witness of the believer, there is no certainty, especially when the unbeliever desires separation (7:15-16).

Having recognized the possibility, and perhaps desirability, of this exception to his general counsel against divorce, Paul reaffirms what he considers to be the norm ("the rule I lay down in all the churches"): that one should remain in the life situation which the Lord has assigned and in which one has been called to faith (7:17). In light of exceptions to general norms throughout this chapter, it is probably unwise to take the phrase "the place in life that the Lord has assigned" too literally and legalistically, as if each person's social or economic or marital status had been predetermined by God. Rather, Paul's view seems to be similar to the one Jesus takes with regard to the situation of the blind man in John 9. His disciples inquire after causes: is the man blind because he sinned or his parents? (9:2). Jesus' response is essentially that the man's blindness is, within the overall purposes of God, an occasion for the work of God to be displayed (9:3).

For Paul, the life situations in which persons are encountered by God's grace and come to faith are situations which, in God's providence, can be transformed and through which the gospel can influence others (such as unbelieving partners).

The principle "remain where you are" is now given broader application to human realities and situations beyond marriage. The one addressed first is that of Jews and Gentiles (7:18-19). The outward circumstances, Paul argues, are of little or no significance ("circumcision is nothing and uncircumcision is nothing"). They neither add to, nor detract from, one's calling into relationship with God, and therefore one's status as Jew or Gentile should not be altered. (It should be noted here that under the pressure of Hellenization, some Jews in the Greek world sought to undo their circumcision [1 Maccabees 1:15]. And we know from both Acts and Galatians that Jewish Christians called for the circumcision of Gentile Christians.)

Once again, it is clear that the general norm, "remain where you are," is not an absolute law. Thus we read in Acts 16:3 that Paul, in light of missionary needs and strategy, had Timothy circumcised even though Timothy was already a believer. Paul's practice in this case would be a direct violation of the rule which he laid down for all the churches (7:17-18), but *only* if that rule had been *intended as an absolute.*

Paul now repeats the rule: "Each one should remain in the situation which he was in when God called him" (7:20), and applies it to yet another situation, namely, that of the slave. Paul does not simply grab a hypothetical situation, for the early church drew a significant number of persons from the lower strata of society (see 1 Cor 1:26-27). So Paul addresses individuals in the congregation who are of the large class of slaves existing throughout the ancient world: "Were you a slave when you were called?" (that is, when you became a Christian). The next words, "Do not let it trouble you," affirm that the authenticity of the person's new life and new status as the Lord's "freedman" (7:21-22) cannot be demeaned and devalued by external circumstances such as social status.

As in the previous applications of the norm ("remain where you are"), Paul immediately allows for a breaking of the norm; indeed, he seems to encourage it: "although if you can gain your freedom, do so" (v. 21; note the RSV rendering: "avail yourself of the opportunity"). As footnotes in some contemporary translations indicate (TEV, RSV), it is possible to translate the Greek of verse 21 with "make use of your present condition instead," meaning that the slave should not take advantage of this opportunity, but rather live as a transformed person within the context of continuing slavery. Some scholars support this rendering, since it would clearly illustrate the norm laid down in the previous verse. However, we have already noted that Paul provides contingencies for much of his instruction in chapter 7, and there is no good reason to doubt that Paul supported the various means for emancipation of individual slaves that were available in the Greco-Roman world.

And yet, Paul's emphasis in the entire chapter, as in the present passage, is his conviction that the most critical issue in human life and relations and institutions is the transformation of persons' lives by God's calling. External circumstances can neither take away from, nor add to, this reality. The instruction to remain in the situation in which one is called to faith (which Paul repeats several more times, in 7:24, 26, 40, and for which he also grants contingencies, in 7:28, 36, 38) can be understood as a missiological principle. To remain in the various situations addressed by Paul in chapter 7 provides opportunity for either unhindered devotion and service to the Lord (7:32-35), or transforming witness toward an unbelieving marriage partner (7:12-

16), or a new way of being present in the context of slavery as one who is free in Christ (7:22-23).

The transforming possibilities of this latter situation are hinted at elsewhere in Paul's writings. Masters who have become believers are called on to deal with their slaves in kindness and to remember that the Master who is over them both sees both as equals (Eph 6:9). The seeds of the liberating gospel are gently sown into the tough soil of slavery. They bore fruit in the lives of Onesimus, the runaway slave, and Philemon, his master. The slave returns to the master, no longer slave but "brother in the Lord" (Philem 15-16).

Note too that the three relational spheres which Paul addresses in chapter 7—male-female, Jew-Gentile (Greek), slave-free—are brought together in that high-water mark of Paul's understanding of the transforming reality of being in Christ: "There is neither Jew nor Greek, slave nor free, male nor female, for you are all one in Christ Jesus" (Gal 3:28). As a rabbi, Paul had given thanks daily, as part of the eighteen benedictions to God, that he had not been born as a Gentile, a slave, a woman. It was his experience of Christ which led him to recognize that these distinctions of superior and inferior were abolished in the new order of things inaugurated in Christ. Surely in this vision the seeds were sown for the ultimate destruction of slavery and all other forms of bondage.

Finally, Paul's understanding of the historical situation in which he and the church found themselves provides another key for his instruction that persons "remain where they are." He, together with most other Christians, was convinced that the eschaton, the climax of God's redemptive intervention, was very near. Statements in 7:26 ("because of the present crisis") and 7:29 ("the time is short") underline that conviction. This belief created a tremendous missionary urgency. The good news had to get out so that as many as possible could yet be saved (see 10:33). This expectation of the imminent end was surely an important factor for the Pauline norm "remain where you are."

(Note: A fuller exploration of Paul's eschatological perspective is given in the following chapter.)

CHAPTER 20

Live As Though You Had No Spouse

What I mean, brothers,
is that the time is short.
From now on those who have wives
should live as if they had none.
1 CORINTHIANS 7:29

What does Paul mean? How can one live with one's spouse "as if" one had none? And why should we have to or want to? How and why is "shortness of time" a factor in favor of living "as if"?

With the phrase "what I mean, brothers," Paul indicates that he is explaining further what he has just said. So let us begin there in the attempt to answer these questions.

In the preceding paragraph (7:25-28), Paul has just counseled single persons, in view of "the present crisis," to remain single (7:26). Should they, however, decide to marry, they would not be sinning (that is, acting contrary to God's purposes; see chapter 17 above). Yet, as married persons, they would "face many troubles in this life," and he wants to spare them this difficult time (7:28).

The reference to difficult experiences in verse 28 is most likely connected with the earlier mention of a "present crisis" (7:26), as well as with the reference to "the time is short" in verse 29. An understanding of the image-world behind these cryptic phrases is imperative if we are to follow Paul's reasoning.

Early Christianity, in continuity with Jesus' teaching about the inbreaking of the kingdom of God and its future consummation, was heir to Jewish understandings of the present and expectations about the future. Their understanding is known as apocalyptic eschatology. The word *eschatology* comes from the Greek words for "last" and "word," and means "teaching about the end." The word *apocalyptic* comes from the Greek word *apocalyptō*, which means "to reveal." Its noun form is *apocalypsis* ("revelation").

Apocalyptic eschatology, as a particular way of understanding the present and envisioning the future, arose in Judaism during the last three centuries B.C. The canonical book of Daniel is its earliest literary expression, which was followed by a host of apocalypses, literary works published in the names of worthy figures in Israel's past, which sought to "reveal" the meaning of Israel's present experience of bondage, deprivation and evil in light of God's purposes. Some of these apocalyptic works were part of the Greek translation of the Hebrew Scriptures, read by Diaspora Jews (that is, Jews living outside Palestine) and later Gentile and Jewish Christians.

The main features of the world view of these visionaries within Israel are the following: (1) the belief that this present age was largely under the control of evil powers; (2) the conviction that the suffering of God's faithful people in this present evil age was a necessary part of the outworking of a divine plan; (3) the certainty that history was quickly moving toward its climax and that the time immediately prior to the cataclysmic destruction of this world and the creation of a new one would be a time of intense tribulation and crisis; (4) the participation, in the outworking of God's purposes, of a transcendent figure seen as one like a man, or the Son of man; (5) the belief that the day of the Lord, the day of his victory over the powers of evil, would be accompanied by the resurrection of the dead (or at least of the righteous dead).

It is clear from the Gospels that Jesus taught and carried on his ministry in light of this Jewish apocalyptic understanding. The battle with evil powers was signaled in his exorcism of demons and interpreted in parables, such as the one about the strong man, whose realm is invaded by one stronger than he (Lk 11:17-22). Satan's power over this present age is breaking (Lk 10:18); the "ruler of this world" shall now be cast out (Jn 12:31). Jesus is the apocalyptic Son of man in whom the reign of God is already breaking into this age, and who will come again to gather his righteous ones (Lk 13:27), raise the dead (Jn 5:28-29) and exercise judgment (Mt 25:31-32). The so-called Olivet discourse, Jesus' teaching about the crisis of the present and the judgment to come (Mk 13; Mt 24—25; Lk 21), conveys a sense of urgency and imminence. And Matthew's account of the signs accompanying Jesus' crucifixion (darkness, earthquake, raisings of the dead—Mt 27:45, 51-53) surely communicates the conviction that this event signaled the coming of the last days.

On the basis of Jesus' life and teaching, his death and resurrection, and the experience of the outpouring of the Spirit at Pentecost (which was perceived as an evidence that the last days had come—Acts 2:14-21), the early church lived under the intense conviction that the final chapter of the scroll of history was being unrolled.

Paul shared this conviction. In his correspondence with the Christians in Thessalonica, he expresses his hope regarding the nearness of the Lord's return (1 Thess 4:13-14), but also reminds them that his return will be preceded by a time of tribulation, the evidence of evil's last struggle to retain control of the world (2 Thess 2). In the cross, the principalities and powers are defeated (Col 2:15). Jesus' resurrection is the downpayment, the first fruits, of the resurrection to come (1 Cor 15:2-23). And because the era of resurrection has already been inaugurated, believers are those who have been transferred from the dominion of darkness into the kingdom of his beloved Son (Col 1:13); they are those on whom the end of the ages has come (1 Cor 10:11). At the same time, believers are participants in the final end-time struggle against the powers of evil (Eph 6:10-18).

Against the background of this world view and within the context of these convictions about living in the last days, Paul's language about "the present crisis" and "the time is short" must be understood. His counsel to the various groups addressed in 1 Corinthians 7 "to remain" in their present relational and institutional contexts, and in those contexts to "live in a right way in undivided devotion to the Lord" (7:35), is eminently appropriate. Life can no longer be lived in its normal, ordinary way "for this world in its present form is passing away" (7:31).

This conviction about the transitional nature of the present determines Paul's thinking about the various arenas of life in 7:29-31. Christians are "new creations" (2 Cor 5:17), and even though they are still living in this world they are no longer of this world (see Jn 17:15-16), but already part of a new order ("the old has gone, the new has come"—2 Cor 5:17). Therefore, "from now on those who have wives should live as if they had none." This statement is followed by four more "as if" contrasts, representative of various areas of life and work and relationships. The point Paul makes is simply that all of life—in light of the fact that Christians are already people of the new creation and that the old order is therefore no longer determinative—must be lived in a new key.

In contrast to the Corinthian spiritualists who wanted to reject marriage, Paul affirms it, but the values and priorities of persons living in this and other human institutions must be kingdom values. There is a higher loyalty than even that to one another in the covenant of marriage. The ordinary structures and expectations which are part of this present order of things—such as the use of power and status to subject others, whether in marriage or social arrangements like slavery—are no longer valid and determinative. Christians are members of a new order while still living in the final days of the old order. And so they should live "as if" the new order had already arrived. And in that new order, even divinely ordained institutions like marriage will be radically transformed.

• C H A P T E R 2 1 •

Many
Gods and
Lords

For even if there are so-called gods,
whether in heaven or on earth
(as indeed there are many "gods"
and "lords"), yet for us
there is but one God.
1 CORINTHIANS 8:5-6

Paul expresses a number of ideas in 1 Corinthians 8:5-6 which, at least on the surface or on first reading, create some inner tension or dissonance. Though in verse 6 he clearly states "there is but one God," a phrase which reaffirms what he has already said in verse 4 ("we know . . . that there is no God but one"), that conviction seems to be qualified by the phrase "for us." Is Paul admitting the existence of divine beings "for others"? A second, corresponding problem is created by Paul's concessive statement "even if there are so-called gods" and the apparent qualification which follows: "as indeed there are many 'gods' and 'lords.' "

These difficulties can be solved once we understand the problem which Paul addresses, the situation in Corinth and Paul's general Jewish-Christian world view.

In chapters 8—10 Paul is apparently addressing a second problem which the church had laid before him in their letter (the first one was addressed in chapter 7; see my discussion in chapters 17-20 above). The question was: Is it permissible for Christians to eat food that has been offered to idols (8:1, 4, 7, 10; 10:14-30)? In light of practices in the pagan world, that question arose in at least three settings. Animals which were sacrificed to pagan divinities at the various temples and shrines were not wholly consumed in the sacrificial flames; often, only certain organs were actually offered. The meat not consumed was sold by the priests to merchants, who resold it to the populace in the meat markets (1 Cor 10:25). The heathen called such meat "sacrificed for sacred purposes" (see 1 Cor 10:28), while Jews and Christians, recognizing idols as the work of human hands (Is 40:18-20), called it "idol-meat" (8:1, 4; 10:19).

In addition to public sacrifices in the temples, there were also sacrificial rituals performed in private homes. Food remaining from such events was then consumed at regular meals. Would Christians invited by their pagan friends or neighbors be contaminated by such food (10:27-28)? Sometimes banquets were held by individuals or associations in temple courts, and Christians could be invited (8:10). Since such meals were associated with the god or gods worshiped in these temples, the question of pagan defilement was very acute, not only for Jewish Christians, but for gentile Christians who were "still so accustomed to idols that when they eat such food they think of it as having been sacrificed to an idol" (8:7).

Within this context the words of Paul in 8:5-6 are to be understood. He affirms, in concert with those believers in Corinth who had arrived at true knowledge, a deeply held and central belief of his Jewish heritage: "There is no God but one"; and because this is the ultimate truth (see Deut 6:4; Is 44:8; 45:5), "an idol is nothing at all in the world" (8:4). From the perspective of both Jewish and Christian convictions (Is 40:18-19; Deut 4:15-19; Rom 1:18-19; Acts 17:29), idols represent no god; they represent nothing at all. That means therefore (at least on the level of true knowledge) that food offered to idols is in essence neutral.

Paul also recognizes, however, that human actions and thoughts and habits are often more shaped and determined by "perceived reality" than by "true reality," by humanly created superstitions than by divine revelations. It is this recognition which stands behind the words about "so-called gods" and "gods and lords."

The words "so-called gods" appear one other time in the New Testament (in 2 Thess 2:4, though "god" is in the singular here), where Paul speaks of "the lawless one" who "will exalt himself over everything that is called God or is worshiped," prior to the coming of the Lord. In both cases, Paul simply recognizes that the pagan world is involved in the belief in, and worship of, gods. Temples to the various Roman and Greek gods in Corinth were ample testimony to this reality. In neighboring Athens, according to Acts 17, Paul addressed the Athenians as "very religious," for he found there many "objects of worship," including an altar "to an unknown god."

Yet, while recognizing this pervasive reality in the pagan world, Paul emphatically qualifies it by claiming that these are only "called" gods. In other words, whatever the degree of reality or unreality assigned to these "objects of worship," what Christians mean by "God" when they speak of the God of Israel and the Father of our Lord Jesus Christ cannot be claimed for these pagan idols.

Having acknowledged the pagan perception concerning the terrestrial and heavenly world as peopled by a host of divinities, and having qualified these as "so-called gods" (8:5), Paul goes on

to acknowledge that even though what pagans worship cannot
be called "God," there is a reality which claims pagan allegiance
and dominates their lives. The statement "there are [indeed]
many 'gods' and many 'lords,' " (8:5) could be interpreted as a further
acknowledgment of the spurious character of all those supposed
beings whom the pagans defined as both "gods" and "lords." That
interpretation would certainly seem to be confirmed by the next
sentence (8:6), where the claim "yet for us there is but one
God . . . and but one Lord" represents the direct Christian coun-
terclaim.

Without setting this view aside, it is also possible that we see
in the phrase "as indeed there are many 'gods' and many 'lords,' "
a reflection of the Jewish and early Christian view of the world
as populated by superterrestrial (not divine!) powers, angels,
demons, largely opposed to God's purposes, enslaving humans
and leading them into idolatry. In 2 Corinthians 4:4 Paul speaks
of the head of this host of spiritual powers as "the god of this
world [who] has blinded the minds of the unbelievers." In Colossians 1:16 and Ephesians 1:21 Christ is pictured as above all
"lordship," and in Ephesians 6:10-11 Christians are seen as those
who are engaged in spiritual struggle with powers that are clearly superterrestrial. It is also clear that Paul acknowledged the
existence of angelic beings (1 Cor 4:9; 6:3), but just as clearly
denounced the worship of such beings (Col 2:18).

In light of this larger view of reality, we can understand why
Paul, in the continuation of the discussion about "meat offered
to idols" in 1 Corinthians 10, maintains that though idols are not
real (10:19), what pagans sacrifice to them they are actually,
unwittingly, offering to demons. The point seems to be that the
evil spirit-powers called demons use the pagans' idolatrous practices to separate the creature from the Creator.

For Paul, there is but one God, the Father, and one Lord, Jesus
Christ (8:6). The designations "gods" and "lords" for the objects

of pagan worship are false and inappropriate. What Christians are to be concerned about, however, are forces and powers of evil against which they must stand "strong in the Lord and in his mighty power" (Eph 6:10).

• C H A P T E R 2 2 •

Headship?

*I want you to realize
that the head of every man is Christ,
and the head of the woman is man,
and the head of Christ is God.*
1 CORINTHIANS 11:3

T hese words in 1 Corinthians 11:3, and two other texts discussed in
the following chapters (23, 24), are easily part of one of the most
difficult and debated passages in all of Paul's epistles. What, precisely, does he mean when he says that "man is the head of
woman"? How are we to understand the assertion of 11:7, which
follows the "head" passage, that man "is the image and glory of
God; but the woman is the glory of man" (the topic of discussion
in chapter 23)? And finally, who are "the angels" in 11:10, due
to whom "the woman ought to have a sign of authority on her
head" (the subject of chapter 24)?

These sayings, because they appear in the same immediate

context (11:2-16) are closely tied to one another; thus in our interpretation we shall occasionally need to refer to matter treated in one or both of the other sayings.

In 11:3 the often heated debate centers on the meaning of the word *head* (which is a literal rendering of the Greek word *kephalē*). For most English readers of the text, the common figurative sense of "head" as ruler, leader, chief, boss, director suggests itself almost immediately. Such an understanding of "head" as connoting "authority over" leads to an interpretation of this text (and of Eph 5:22-23; see chapter 34 below) as Paul's teaching about hierarchical order in the relation between men and women. Some who stand within this interpretive tradition go so far as to posit a "chain of command," where authority is passed along: from God to Christ to man to woman.

While the NIV, RSV, NASB and NEB are cautious in their translation, rendering the Greek *kephalē* with its literal English equivalent "head," other contemporary versions opt for a figurative meaning. Thus the TEV renders *kephalē* with "supreme over." The Living Bible's paraphrase becomes even more interpretive in this particular direction when it renders the text: "a wife is responsible to her husband, her husband is responsible to Christ, and Christ is responsible to God."

Even when such explicit *interpretations* of the term *kephalē* are not employed, the literal "head," as in NIV, implicitly suggests an interpretation along the same lines because of the common understanding of "head" in English when applied to persons in relationships such as marriage or other institutions. Common phrases like "she is head of the division" or "he is the head of his family" illustrate this everyday metaphorical meaning of "head" in our language.

Apart from the question whether this common English meaning is also the common Greek meaning of "head" when used figuratively, serious issues are raised by such an interpretation.

How are we to see the relation between Christ and God? If God occupies a rank superior to Christ, then we have here a revival of the ancient heresy of "subordinationism" and a challenge to the classical doctrine of the Trinity.

Further, if husbands (or men; the Greek word is the same) are under the authority of Christ, and wives (or women; the same Greek word) are under the authority of husbands/men, do we then not have a situation where women stand only in indirect relation to Christ, via their husbands? Such a conclusion is in fact reached by some when they understand the series (God — Christ — Man — Woman) as indicating a "growing distance from God," or by others who extend the "chain of command" to children (on the basis of Eph 5:21—6:4) and maintain that the woman's authority over her children is a "derived" authority; that is, she exercises that authority "on behalf of" her husband.

The core issue in our attempt to grasp Paul's instruction is this: what meaning, or meanings, did the word *kephalē* have in the common Greek language of the New Testament period? How would Greek-speaking Christians in Corinth have heard Paul when he used *kephalē*? And how did the hearing of *kephalē* in 11:3 help them understand Paul's instructions concerning appropriate decorum in their public worship (11:4-16)? To answer these questions attention will be given to linguistic data, Paul's use of *kephalē* elsewhere in his epistles, and the thrust of his argument in 11:2-16.

The linguistic evidence points strongly, if not overwhelmingly, away from the common reading of "head" as "chief," "ruler," "authority over," though there are many conservative scholars who would challenge this. The most exhaustive Greek-English Lexicon covering Greek literature from about 900 B.C. to A.D. 600, among numerous metaphorical meanings for *kephalē*, does not give a single definition which would indicate that in common ordinary Greek usage, *kephalē* included the meaning "superior rank" or "supreme over" or "leader" or "authority."

What is especially interesting in this lexicographic evidence is that in the 1897, eighth revised edition of this lexicon, the final entry under "metaphorical" meanings is "of persons, *a chief.*"[1] But not a single citation from the literature is given to support or illustrate such a definition. Therefore, in light of the lack of evidence, that definition is not included in the later editions. However, among the range of meanings which *kephalē* had in ordinary Greek were "origin" or "source" or "starting point" and "crown" or "completion" or "consummation." As we shall see below, these meanings of *kephalē* do far greater justice to the Pauline usages of *kephalē* than the "authority" nuances conveyed by the English "head."

Strong support for the linguistic evidence (that is, that the metaphorical range of meanings of *kephalē* did not normally include the ideas of "authority over" or "superior rank") comes from the Greek translation of the Hebrew Scriptures (commonly called the Septuagint) made approximately between 250-150 B.C. by a large group of Jewish scholars for the Jews living outside Palestine whose first, and sometimes only, language was Greek.

Like the English word "head" and the Greek word *kephalē,* the Hebrew word *ro'sh* has first of all the literal meaning "head of man or beast." But like English and Greek, it also has numerous figurative meanings. In an exhaustive study of how the Septuagint translators rendered the Hebrew word *ro'sh,*[2] the following data emerged. In the more than 200 times when *ro'sh* refers to a physical head, the translators almost always used *kephalē.* About 180 times, *ro'sh* clearly has the figurative meaning of "leader" or "chief" or "authority figure" of a group. There is thus a close similarity between the English "head" and the Hebrew *ro'sh;* figuratively, both frequently designate an authority figure.

When the translators, however, sought the appropriate Greek word to render this figurative meaning, they used not *kephalē,* but archōn (and its derivatives) in the great majority of cases (138 times). Archōn means "ruler," "commander," "leader." Its derivatives include meanings such as "authority," "chief," "captain," "prince," "chief of tribe," "head of family." Most of the remaining occurrences of ro'sh (when it designates an authority figure) are translated by several other specific Greek words (such as hēgeomai, "to have dominion over"). In only eight out of 180 cases was kephalē used to translate ro'sh when it designated the leader or ruler of a group. It is very possible that one of the figurative meanings of kephalē (namely, "top" or "crown") allowed the translator to use it in describing a prominent individual. It may also be that in these few cases one of the Septuagint translators simply used the literal equivalent for ro'sh, namely kephalē (since both mean "head"). This is in fact what happens all too frequently in any translation when it is too literal. The exact equivalent may, in fact, distort the meaning conveyed by the original in its own context.

It is clear from this data that the Greek translators were keenly aware that kephalē did not normally have a metaphorical meaning equivalent to that of ro'sh; else they would have used it for most, if not all, occurrences of ro'sh when it carried the meaning "chief" or "leader."

This linguistic evidence, which suggests that the idea of "authority over" was not native to the Greek kephalē, has led numerous scholars to see behind Paul's use of "head" either the meaning "source, origin" or "top, crown, completion."[3]

Another factor to take into consideration is that nowhere else in the New Testament is kephalē used to designate a figure of authority. If that had been a prominent meaning, it could have served well in numerous places in the Gospels where the head or master of a household appears; yet kephalē is never used to convey this meaning (see, for example, Mt 10:25; 13:52; Lk 13:25; 14:21).

If the readers of Paul's Greek did not hear our "headship" concept in the word *kephalē*, but rather the idea of "source, origin," what did it convey to them, and how did that meaning in 11:3 lay the foundation for Paul's admonitions about appropriate hair length and decorum in public worship? Cyril of Alexandria, an important Greek-speaking leader of the church in the fourth century, commenting on this text wrote: "Thus we say that the *kephalē* of every man is Christ, because he was excellently made through him. And the *kephalē* of woman is man, because she was taken from his flesh. Likewise, the *kephalē* of Christ is God, because he is from him according to nature."[4]

This interpretation meets all the requirements of the passage and its context, and at the same time sheds light on several other of Paul's statements where both Christ and the man are designated as "head" of something or someone (Eph 4:15; 5:23; Col 1:15-20; 2:19). Paul, as other New Testament writers, affirms Christ as the one by whom all things were created (Col 1:16; 1 Cor 8:6; Jn 1:3). Thus Paul can say that Christ, as God's agent of creation, gave the first man, and thus every man, life ("Christ is the source of man's life"). Such a meaning is confirmed by the fact that in the same passage (vv. 7-9) he clearly has the creation narrative of Genesis 1—2 in mind. Though it is obvious that, in a final sense, Christ/God is also the source of the woman's life (v. 12), Paul is here considering the sequence of creation of the human species in Genesis 2.

This temporal, sequential thought continues in the sentence, "And the head of the woman is man" (that is, "the man is the source of woman's life"). According to Genesis 2:21-23 Adam is the origin of Eve's being. And it is precisely this Old Testament text which Paul has in mind (vv. 8, 12). That "source" is the appropriate meaning of *kephalē* in 11:3 is confirmed by Paul's "source" language in his appeal to Genesis 2.

Behind this temporal sequence stands God ("everything comes

from God"— verse 12—that is, God is the source of everything;
see 1 Cor 8:6). Therefore, "the head of Christ is God" (that is,
the source of Christ's being is God). Cyril of Alexandria said, "the
kephalē of Christ is God because he is *from* him according to nature" (emphasis mine). Though Cyril's language reflects the later
trinitarian discussion, his affirmation is solidly grounded in the
New Testament. According to John 1:1-14, the Word, which was
God and was with God, came forth and became flesh in the
Incarnation. In John 8:42, 13:3 and 16:27 Jesus is said to have
come *from* God.

On the basis of the data discussed above, it would seem best
to translate 11:3 as follows: "I want you to understand that
Christ is the source of man's being; the man is the source of
woman's being; and God is the source of Christ's being." When
read like this, it lays a solid foundation for, and sheds light on,
the rest of the passage (11:4-16), in which our next two "hard
sayings" are located.

Notes

[1]Henry George Liddell and Robert Scott, *A Greek-English Lexicon*, 2 vols.,
rev. H. S. Jones & R. McKenzie (Oxford: Clarendon Press, 1940), 1:944-
45.
[2]Berkeley and Alvera Mickelsen, "What Does *kephalē* Mean in the New
Testament?" in *Women, Authority & the Bible*, ed. Alvera Mickelsen
(Downers Grove, Ill.: InterVarsity Press, 1986), pp. 97-110.
[3]See, for example, Stephen Bedale, "The Meaning of *Kephalē* in the Pauline Epistles," *Journal of Theological Studies* n.s. 5 (1954): 211-215; C. K.
Barrett, *The First Epistle to the Corinthians* (New York: Harper & Row,
1968). H. N. Ridderbos, *Paul: An Outline of Theology*, trans. J. Richard
deWitt (Grand Rapids, Mich.: Eerdmans, 1975), pp. 379-82; S. Scott
Bartchy, "Power, Submission, and Sexual Identity among the Early
Christians," in *Essays on New Testament Christianity*, ed. C. R. Wetzel (Cin-
cinnati: Standard Publishing, 1978), pp. 50-80.
[4]G. W. Lampe, *A Patristic Greek Lexicon* (Oxford University Press, 1968),
p. 749.

• C H A P T E R 2 3 •

The
Glory
of Man

A man ought not to cover his head,
since he is the image
and glory of God;
but the woman is the glory of man.
1 CORINTHIANS 11:7

Once again, *as it appears also in 11:3, Paul seems to put women* one step further removed from God than men. Why is man said to be the glory of God, while woman is the glory of man? Why are women not also said to be the glory of God? And does the fact that God's image is affirmed for man, but not for woman, mean that only the male half of the species is made in God's image? And what does covering of one's head (with a veil or one's hair) have to do with being or reflecting someone's glory?

We begin our attempt to respond to these questions by looking

The previous chapter on 1 Corinthians 11:3 should be read as background for this chapter.

at the broader context of our passage, and then moving on to a careful examination of the details within the thrust of Paul's thought.

In chapters 8—10 of this letter, Paul has been dealing with the issue of Christian liberty in light of both true knowledge ("correct beliefs"), caring love for one's fellow believers, and concern for living and acting in ways which "build up" others or the church. That is, Christian freedom with respect to externals—to rules and regulations, to forms of ritual and ceremony—is not an absolute freedom. Christian freedom, based on the liberating grace of God, is freedom for the other, for the other's good, for the growth of the fellowship in love and faith and hope.

Paul sums up this discussion in 10:31 with these words: "whatever you do, do all for the glory of God." How do we live and act for the glory of God? By not causing "anyone to stumble, whether Jews, Greeks or the church of God. . . . For I am not seeking my own good but the good of many, so that they may be saved" (10:32-33). Both with respect to the outside world and the fellowship, this principle of Christian behavior is the source for Paul's specific instructions which follow.

Concerns about propriety with regard to appearance in the context of public worship are addressed first (11:2-16). This is followed by a severe criticism of their misunderstanding of the nature of the Lord's Supper and its consequence in their actions (11:17-34). Finally, Paul addresses the use and misuse of the gifts of the Spirit (12:1—14:40). In each of these situations, the principle for Christian action laid down in 10:31-33 must be kept in mind.

What precisely is the problem regarding proper appearance for worship in 11:2-16? As frequently is the case in this "occasional" letter, we must make deductions from Paul's answers. From 11:4-5 we may assume that social, cultural or ritual norms were being ignored or deliberately set aside in the context of worship.

It is possible that their libertine enthusiasm, which had led them to a demeaning or total rejection of male-female sexuality and distinctions (see 1 Cor 7), had also led them to reject other cultural and religious norms. Thus, perhaps in a deliberate attempt to wipe out distinctions, some men may have worn a head covering in worship (11:4), while some women rejected the covering prescribed for them by cultural or religious conventions (11:5).

Though the Greek word for "veil" does not appear in this text (and therefore some commentators have argued that Paul is here speaking only of hair as a covering), it is best to understand the phrase "having [something] down from the head" (11:4) to refer to a head covering which concealed the hair and shoulders. Verse 6 seems to confirm this sense, where "not covering the head" is likened to shaving or cutting the hair short. The sense seems to be: "if you are not going to cover (veil) your head, you might as well cut off your hair; it amounts to the same thing!"

Why does a man who prays and prophesies with his head *covered* dishonor his head (11:4), while a woman who prays and prophesies with her head *uncovered* dishonor her head (11:5-6)? The answer to this question is cryptically given in our "hard saying" in 11:7. But in order to understand that answer, the problem as articulated in 11:4-6 needs some unraveling.

What do the phrases "dishonors his/her head" in verses 4 and 5 mean? The first uses of "head" in these sentences ("with his head covered" and "with her head uncovered") are obviously references to their "physical heads." Does "head" in the phrases "dishonor his/her head" refer also to their physical heads or to their "figurative heads" given in 11:3 (Christ, of the man; the man, of the woman)? Commentators are fairly divided, with some holding that both meanings may be intended.

In either or both cases, dishonor is the result. When a man wears a covering on his head, it is as if he wore long hair; but long hair on men is against "nature" (11:4). For Paul, as in pop-

ular Greek philosophy, cultural customs were perceived as exten-
sions of natural law (and for Paul, more specifically God's created
order of things). Therefore, wearing a covering was against
God's purposes. It demeans God's design and thus dishonors
both God and man. Woman's long hair—also designed "by nature" (that is, God)—is her glory (11:15). To uncover it is the
same as cutting it off. That disgraces her, since her very being
is demeaned. It may also disgrace her "figurative" head (that is,
her husband), since appearing in public without a covering brings
reproach on him from the society (especially if, as some have
argued, it was the practice of prostitutes and other libertines in
Corinth to move in public without a covering).

In light of Paul's principle for Christian life—to act in ways
which lead to the good, the salvation of as many as possible
(10:32-33)—he is concerned that Christians maintain the kind of
public worship which does not bring disgrace through unacceptable, shameful practices. The church was God's alternative to
broken Corinthian society (see chapter 14 above). Its flouting of
contemporary cultural conventions could bring social criticism
and hinder the gospel.

Yet Paul is much more than a pragmatist. He grounds his
reasoning in an understanding of God's revealed intention. This
intention is focused in 11:7, though its foundation is already laid
in 11:3. If, as we have argued (in chapter 22 above), Paul's use
of the Greek word *kephalē* ("head") is to be understood not in
terms of our idea of "headship" (that is, authority over), but
rather in terms of "source/origin," then a central, unifying theme
in his argument emerges.

Paul's guiding principle for Christian conduct (10:32-33) is
grounded in the even higher principle: "whatever you do, do it
all for the glory of God" (10:31). Since the word *glory* appears
three more times in the passage which follows (11:7, 15), we can
assume that the manifestation of God's glory and human partic-

ipation in that glory is a central purpose of community worship.

In biblical thought, that which is made, or emerges out of another, manifests or reflects the glory of its maker or origin. Thus, "the heavens are telling the glory of God; and the firmament proclaims his handiwork" (Ps 19:1). The worshiper is exhorted to declare God's glory (Ps 96:3-8) and stands under judgment when God's glory is perverted in false worship and distorted human living (Rom 1:22-32). According to both John and Paul, Jesus' life reflected God's glory (Jn 1:14; 13:31-32; 17:4; Col 1:27). Since in Christ the fullness of God expressed itself (Col 1:19), Paul could say that "the light of the knowledge of the glory of God [was revealed] in the face of Christ" (2 Cor 4:6). Not only that, but Christ is the very "image of God" (2 Cor 4:4).

This complex of ideas seems to stand behind the language and ideas in 11:7. Insofar as the man is the result of God's creative work (Gen 1:26; 2:7) and has his existence out of Christ (11:3), who is the glory and image of God, "he is the image and glory of God" (11:7). And insofar as the woman has her existence out of the man (Gen 2:21-23; 1 Cor 11:3), she "is the glory of man" (11:7).

What Paul does not say in this context is important. He does not say that woman is the image of man; she is only his glory. For Paul knew that, according to Genesis 1:26-27, human beings as male and female were created in God's image. He is also clear that both the man and the woman have their being ultimately out of God's being as a result of God's creative act (11:12). Thus the woman as man's glory is only a recognition of the temporal sequence of God's creative activity, since her being is derived from the being of Adam. But no less than man, woman is the glory and image of God since she too is "from God" (11:12).

The purpose of worship is to glorify God. In contexts where cultural-religious norms and customs for proper attire and length of hair were understood as reflecting, at least to some extent, the order of "nature" (11:14-15),[1] the rejection of those customs in the worship of the church in Corinth undermined the purpose of worship. A "covered" man or an "uncovered" woman would bring dishonor rather than glory. It is this concern which motivates Paul's thought in this difficult passage.

Notes

[1]See the discussion of this matter in C. K. Barrett, *The First Epistle to the Corinthians* (New York: Harper & Row, 1968), pp. 256-57.

• C H A P T E R 2 4 •

Because
of the
Angels

*For this reason, and because
of the angels, the woman ought
to have a sign of authority on her head.*
1 CORINTHIANS 11:10

Who are "the angels," *because of whom women are "to have a sign
of authority"* on their heads when praying and prophesying?
Why should they be interested in women's appearance in worship? What is the "sign of authority" on a woman's head, and
whose authority does it signify?

In the discussion of 11:3 and 11:7 we saw that Paul argued for
the appropriateness of women praying and prophesying in public
worship with a head covering for both practical evangelistic reasons and biblical-theological considerations. Now he adds yet another dimension to the discussion. The opening words of the
sentence, "For this reason," are most naturally a reference to the

preceding discussion and the reasons already given for the propriety of a woman's head covering. Some see this statement as pointing forward to the phrase "on account of the angels." A good example is the TEV, which reads, "on account of the angels, then, a woman should have a covering." To take it in that way would make the whole prior discussion, with its various reasons for a head covering, meaningless.

Why is "because of the angels" another reason for the observance of the custom? What do angels have to do with the situation? Because of the obscurity of this statement, various interpretations have been offered throughout the church's history.

Among early church fathers the interpretation of the "angels" as priests or bishops was prominent. The Greek word *angelos* literally means "messenger" and could refer to a human messenger in the sense of an envoy, one who is sent. Thus the "angel of the church in Ephesus" (as well as the other "angels" of the churches addressed in Revelation 2—3) were held to be the bishops of those churches. From this the conclusion was drawn that the "angels" in 11:10 referred to visiting leaders from other churches, who would be offended by women's inappropriate appearance in worship.

This interpretation is unsatisfactory because nowhere in Paul's epistles, or the rest of the Epistles, is the word *angelos* ever used as a designation of a church leader. In all but one case, Paul uses the word exclusively for supernatural, spiritual beings, the servants of God. The one exception is Galatians 4:14, where it is a self-designation: "You welcomed me as if I were an angel of God." Since it is used as an analogy, it really belongs to the category of Paul's normal usage.

A second line of interpretation sees these "angels" as a threat to women, against which the head covering in worship protects them. On the basis of Genesis 6:2-4, where it is said that the "sons of God" were attracted by the beauty of human females and impregnated them, Jewish traditions arose which interpreted these "sons of God" as angelic beings, who, as fallen angels, lusted after women. There are numerous passages in the non-canonical intertestamental literature[1] which build on the Genesis narrative and speculate on the danger to humanity from these fallen angels. This linkage of 11:10 with Genesis 6 and subsequent speculation is at best problematic. There is no indication whatever in our text that Paul is concerned about women's protection from evil angelic beings. And how would the veil, while praying or prophesying, protect against their lustful advances?

A third interpretation, which seems more fruitful as a context for Paul's cryptic allusion, sees behind the reference "because of the angels," the common Jewish belief that God's servants, the angels, are present especially in the worship of God's people. In Psalm 138:1 the worshiper exclaims: "I give thanks to thee, O God; before the gods I sing thy praise." These "gods" were understood as heavenly beings, servants in the divine court and guardians of the created order. Hebrews reflects these ideas when it envisions the ultimate context of worship, the heavenly Jerusalem where God and "innumerable angels in joyful assembly" are present (12:22). Paul elsewhere posits angels as observers of human conduct as well (1 Cor 4:9).

A more specific background for our text from Judaism is to be found in the Qumran writings, commonly known as the Dead Sea Scrolls. J. A. Fitzmyer has shown that these Jewish sectarians believed that angels were present when the community assembled for worship, and that they would be offended by any acts which transgressed created order.[2] Paul confirms the presence of such a belief in a word addressed to Timothy: "in the presence of God and of Christ and of the elect angels I charge you to keep these rules" (1 Tim 5:21). We have here, as in 11:3, the connection between worship, congregational norms and angels who are present.

If, in light of this background, the angels of 11:10 are to be understood as guardians of those orders which are according to "the very nature of things" (11:14), then women's uncovered heads would be an infringement on that order. Thus, "because of the angels, the woman ought to have a sign of authority on her head."

We are still left with the questions: What constitutes the "sign of authority"? Why "authority"? and Whose authority?

The text reads literally: "The woman ought to have authority on the head." Because of the emphasis on a head covering in the context, one would have expected Paul to say, "The woman ought to have a head covering." This expectation in fact caused some early church fathers to replace the word "authority" with the word "veil." The identification between the head covering and "authority on the head" seems certain (note the RSV decision to translate, "That is why a woman ought to have a veil on her head, because of the angels"). By using the word *authority* (the Greek *exousia*—"authority," "power," "right"), Paul apparently intends to interpret the significance of the covering for the woman's participation in the prayer life and prophetic ministry of the congregation.

Since the head covering cannot by itself possess authority, some commentators and translations have opted for "a sign of authority" (that is, the veil is a sign for something else); examples are the NIV and NEB (NASB renders "symbol of authority"). Such a rendering leaves open the questions "authority for what?" and "whose authority?" In my judgment, both the TEV and the Living Bible paraphrases go significantly beyond both the textual and contextual evidence. The TEV translates: "a woman should have a covering over her head to show that she is under her husband's authority." That translation decision answers the questions posed above by giving the husband authority over the wife. The Living Bible interprets essentially the same way, except

that it generalizes the concept of authority: not only is the wife
to be under the authority of her husband, but "woman . . . is
under man's authority."

These readings of the text presuppose two things and then
import them into the text: (1) They assume that the relationship
between man/husband and woman/wife as posited in 11:3 is a
relationship of "authority over," and that this "principle of headship" determines all aspects of the rest of the passage (11:4-16).
I have attempted to show (see chapter 22 above) that such a
reading of 11:3 is likely incorrect. (2) They assume that the head
covering is in fact a symbol of the husband's authority over his
wife. Yet no convincing proof of this assumption exists. A parallel has been sought in the Greek word *basileia*, which usually
means "kingship" or "kingdom," but also can have the meaning
"royal crown"; and the crown was a "sign of royal power/author-
ity." This supposed parallel breaks down when we recognize that
here the power and authority of the wearer is meant, and not
that of another person.

In view of these problems with the rather common interpretation discussed above, the text needs to be read much more
literally. What really does Paul say? The text reads: "the woman
should have *exousia* ('power,' 'right,' 'authority') on the head." By
choosing the word *exousia* rather than "head covering," Paul
seems to suggest that by wearing the covering—and thus con-
forming her outward appearance with "nature/custom"—the
woman has authority. Such an understanding of the text is
strongly supported by recent studies.[3]

Authority for what? is the final question. We have seen that
the ultimate purpose of worship is to give glory to God. A part
of the way by which the glory of God is reflected is through the
prayers of the worshipers and the proclamation of the gospel.
Now since the woman has her origin in the man and thus reflects
his glory (see chapter 23 above), she ought to wear a head cov-

ering in worship in order to conceal "man's glory" and therefore
be in a position to reflect the glory of God in praying and prophesying. By being veiled, women would not distract attention from
the worship of God and avoid accusations of disgraceful behavior.

At the same time, the covering also represents her God-given
right to bring glory to God through praying and prophesying, a
gift of the Spirit (see Acts 2:17-18) which transcends former
religious and cultural limitations imposed on women in public
worship. As Walter Liefeld has shown, Paul used the word *exousia*
("authority") five times within the larger context of 1 Corinthians 8—14, always in the sense of Christian freedom from externals for the sake of others and the progress of the gospel.[4] By
linking this same concept with the woman's covering he is, at one
and the same time, affirming the need for restraint regarding
externals and her right (authority) to participate in that which
is essential; namely, the expression of her direct relation to God
in prayer and the exercise of the gift of prophetic proclamation
for the edification of the church and the glory of God.

This understanding of the text leads naturally to the next two
verses. The statement that "in the Lord" man and woman are
interdependent and complementary (11:11-12) has often been
taken to represent a halfhearted concession by Paul. In light of
the interpretation of the previous verses which has been offered,
verses 11-12 are a ringing affirmation that in the new era which
has been inaugurated (that is, "in the Lord"), despite the need for
temporal limitations, man and woman have their being in God
("everything comes from God") and are called to do everything
"for the glory of God" (10:31).

Notes

[1] See the passages in the following books of the Pseudepigrapha: Eth
Enoch 6-7, 67-78; Testament of Reuben 5; Jubilees 5; Apoc of Baruch
56:8-13.

[2]See Joseph A. Fitzmyer, "A Feature of Qumran Angelology and the Angels of I Corinthians 11:10," *New Testament Studies* 4 (1957-1958): 45-58.

[3]M. D. Hooker, "Authority on Her Head: An Examination of I Corinthians 11:10," *New Testament Studies* 10 (1963-1964): 410-16. Walter L. Liefeld, "Women, Submission & Ministry in 1 Corinthians" in *Women, Authority & the Bible*, ed. Alvera Mickelsen (Downers Grove, Ill.: Inter-Varsity Press, 1986), pp. 145-46. C. K. Barrett, *1 Corinthians*, pp. 254-55. William F. Orr and James Arthur Walther, *I Corinthians*, The Anchor Bible, vol. 32 (New York: Doubleday, 1976), pp. 260-64.

[4]Liefeld, "Women, Submission & Ministry," pp. 145-46.

· C H A P T E R 2 5 ·

Discerning
the
Body

For anyone who eats and drinks
without recognizing the body
of the Lord eats and drinks
judgment on himself.
1 CORINTHIANS 11:29

T he ominous words of *1 Corinthians 11:29 are written by Paul right*
after he reminds his readers of the tradition about the institution
of the Lord's Supper (or Eucharist) and the words of interpretation which Jesus gave as he broke bread and passed the cup on
the night before the crucifixion (11:23-26). These words were
usually spoken before the celebration of the Lord's Supper in the
churches where I grew into adolescence and adulthood. The
emotions which they called forth from me were not only a sense
of seriousness and awe, but also, and perhaps overwhelmingly,
a sense of fear. What if I did not properly discern or recognize
"the body of the Lord"? How would, or could, I make sure that

in my eating of the bread and drinking of the cup I would not sin "against the body and blood of the Lord"? (11:27; this warning comes just before our hard saying and is followed by the admonition, "a man ought to examine himself . . .").

The fear of "sinning against" and "not discerning" at times caused me to avoid participation in the Supper or to stay away from worship altogether on those Sundays when Communion was celebrated. In some Christian traditions, these warnings and admonitions have been used to exclude persons from the celebration who are identified as having committed particular sins and are thus "unworthy" to partake of the elements.

The criterion of "worthiness," whether self-imposed or imposed by others, is really the crux of this passage. What makes one worthy and thus not subject to judgment? And if one's worthiness is related to moral-ethical perfection or spiritual maturity, can anyone ever qualify to participate at the Lord's table? These questions are particularly troublesome since they arise from a text related to the celebration of that event—the passion of our Lord—where God's unconditional love for sinners is revealed (see Rom 5:8, "While we were yet sinners, Christ died for us").

For me it was amazingly liberating to discover, after giving greater attention to the problem which Paul was addressing in Corinth and the special terms he used, that my fears were not warranted; that the celebration was indeed a powerful reminder that Christ gave his life to save sinners like me; that it was a challenge to discern, again and again, the significance of his death for my own life. Let us briefly explore the context of this passage and Paul's terminology to really hear the intended Word for the Corinthians and for us.

The larger context for our saying begins at 11:17, and it is clear from Paul's introductory words ("In the following directions . . .") that he is moving away from a discussion of women's

decorum at worship (11:3-16) to deal with a second problem in
their life as a gathered congregation. What is that problem? Paul
shoots rather straight: "Your meetings do more harm than good"
(11:17). Then he proceeds to articulate the nature of the harm
that results when they "come together as a church." He has
heard that "there are divisions" among them and that these divisions manifest themselves precisely at the point where they
"come together" (11:18, 20).

What a paradox! Were they not, as a gathered fellowship, the
temple of God's Spirit (3:16)? And wasn't the Spirit the one who
had incorporated them, as diverse a group as they were, "into
one body . . . so that there should be no division in the body, but
that its parts should have equal concern for each other" (12:13,
25)? Paul's vision for the fellowship of God's people in Corinth
was far from being realized. Indeed, at the very occasion where
one would have expected the greatest realization of that vision
for mutuality and caring—at their common meals—they manifested a haughty, individualistic disregard for others.

In the verses which follow the introductory charge (11:20-26),
it is apparent that the occasion at which their divisions manifest
themselves is an ordinary meal which includes symbolic actions
and the recital of significant words. These festal occasions came
to be known as the *agapē*, or love feasts (see Jude 12; 2 Peter 2:13).
What was to be central—a caring love for one another grounded
in Christ's sacrificial death—was manifestly absent: "When you
come together, it is not the Lord's Supper which you eat" (11:20).
Rather, they were eating and drinking in an individualistic, selfish manner (11:21). Some, apparently the more affluent among
them, had brought their food and, without waiting for others,
had gone ahead and eaten their meals. There was even excessive
drinking of the wine. All of this took place while the poorer
members of the fellowship, who were able to bring little or nothing, were humiliated (11:22). Rather than sharing out of their

abundance (as the Jerusalem Christians had done; Acts 4:32), those of means acted as if they were in their own homes. It was not the Lord's Supper they were eating, but their own!

Having laid bare the irregularity at their love feasts, which he describes as a "despising of the church of God" (11:22), Paul reminds them of the words which Jesus spoke at his last meal with the disciples (11:23-25). In those words, symbolically represented in broken bread and poured-out wine, Jesus interpreted the significance of his life and death: it was for them (11:24); a new covenant had been inaugurated through the sacrifice of his shed blood (11:25); they had become participants in that new covenant community, as Paul had already reminded them earlier ("Because there is one loaf, we who are many are one body"— 10:17). When they ate and drank, and heard the words of the Lord, they were to "remember" him. Their eating and drinking was to be a declaration and proclamation of the Lord's self-sacrifice (11:26).

Some commentators understand the emphasis on "remembering" the Lord and "proclaiming" his suffering servanthood on our behalf as a special call to discipleship and the imitation of Jesus. In light of Paul's teachings elsewhere (for example, "Be imitators of God as beloved children and walk in love, as Christ loved us and gave himself up for us"—Eph 5:1), this is surely what Paul wanted the believers in Corinth to be about. Instead, they were eating the bread of the Lord and drinking the cup of the Lord "in an unworthy manner" (11:27).

Thus the issue for Paul is *not* the "worthiness" of individuals. If that were the case, none would ever be "worthy." Rather, they were participating in the Lord's Supper in an unworthy manner by demonstrating contempt for the community as a whole, by actions which were not controlled by love for the needy brothers and sisters. In this action, they are "guilty of sinning against the body and blood of the Lord" (11:27).

The phrase "guilty of sinning against" (NIV) translates the Greek word *enochos*. It is used mostly as a legal term, meaning "liable for," "answerable for," or "guilty." The thrust of Paul is then that those who eat and drink unworthily (in the sense indicated above) are guilty of Christ's sacrificial death. They oppose and contradict in their loveless behavior the purpose of Christ's death, namely, to create a new covenant community which will model, in the midst of a fragmented, broken world, a new way of servanthood which seeks the good of others.

It is within the context of these concerns of Paul and this understanding of the meaning of their *agapē* meals that the admonition to "self-examination" (11:28) and properly "recognizing the body of the Lord" (11:29) must be heard. The Corinthians are to examine themselves with regard to the spirit in which they approach their participation: Is it other-directed or self-centered?

Some of the earliest and best Greek manuscripts do not have the phrase "of the Lord." It is therefore quite probable that Paul's original letter simply read, "recognize the body." But in either case, the context indicates that Paul is speaking about that reality which elsewhere he designates either "body" or "one body" or "the body of Christ" (see 1 Cor 10:17; 12:12-13, 27; Eph 2:16; 3:6; 4:4; Col 1:18). Not discerning the body (or the body of the Lord) is to fundamentally misunderstand the nature of Christian community and act in ways which undermine its vitality, its life and witness. It is that which stands under God's judgment, for to do harm to Christ's body is to oppose the purposes of God for which the Lord's body was broken and his life's blood was poured out.

• CHAPTER 26 •

Should We All Speak in Tongues?

*I would like every one of you
to speak in tongues,
but I would rather have
you prophesy.*
1 CORINTHIANS 14:5

Paul's words in 1 Corinthians 14:5 and the surrounding discussion of the presence and function of spiritual gifts in individual believers and the church have raised numerous questions: What is the place of "speaking in tongues" in the church? Are those who have experienced this gift more spiritual Christians, more open to the Spirit's working, than those who have not? Is Paul's point that all Christians should have this gift? Or is it rather that all should participate in prophetic work, assigning a negligible place to "speaking in tongues"?

Some Christians, on the basis of this and other texts, have come to feel superior, or more complete, because they have the gift of tongues, and wished with Paul that their brothers and sisters could have this same rich experience. Other Christians, on the basis of the same texts, consider glossolalia (from the Greek *glōssai*—"tongues") a manifestation of primitive, immature faith and consider the absence of this gift or experience a mark of greater maturity. Still others, seeing the lively, enthusiastic faith and witness of some who have the gift of tongues, feel somehow not quite in tune with God's Spirit and earnestly desire or seek an experience of the Spirit which would bring vitality into an otherwise static faith.

These concerns and positions—which have been present in parts of the church to some degree throughout church history—have come to the fore again more recently in what has become known as the charismatic movement (from the Greek *charisma*—"gift"). Since this movement has crossed denominational boundaries and influenced believers in virtually all Christian traditions, it is particularly important that we come to understand this hard saying.

A brief definition of Paul's terms will help. The two activities which are contrasted in our saying are "speaking in tongues" and "prophesying." The phenomenon of "tongues," which Paul identifies as a gift (Greek, *charisma*) of the Spirit (in 1 Cor 12—14), must be clearly distinguished from the phenomenon which accompanied the outpouring of the Spirit at Pentecost (in Acts 2:1-12).

In Acts, the Spirit enabled Jesus' disciples to "speak in other tongues" (*glōssai*—Acts 2:4, 11) in such a way that the audience, made up of peoples from various language groups throughout the Greco-Roman world, heard them speak in their own languages (Greek, *dialekton*—"dialect/language") the good news of Jesus (2:6, 8). Here it is clear that a miraculous speaking and hearing is indicated in which intelligible meaning is articulated and perceived. Peter's interpretation of this phenomenon also shows that it is to be taken as intelligible proclamation of the wonders of God. He cites the prophecy of Joel 2:28-32, where the outpouring of the Spirit leads to prophetic proclamation (Acts 2:17-18).

In Corinth, on the other hand, the phenomenon of tongues with which Paul is concerned is identified as "unintelligible utterance": no one understands it (14:2); it needs to be interpreted if it is to benefit the church (14:5); it is contrasted with "intelligible words" (14:9, 19) and "all sorts of languages . . . none of them without meaning" (14:10); it does not involve the mind (14:14); others won't know what is being said (14:16).

With this gift of "tongues" Paul contrasts the gift of "prophecy." We must be careful at the outset not to read a limited idea into this word. The word does not mean simply "predicting the future." Prophesying sometimes included this predictive element (both among O.T. and Christian prophets), but this aspect is neither exclusive nor primary. The prophets of Israel primarily addressed the word of God to their people's present reality. This is also the primary aspect of prophetic proclamation in early Christianity.

In Acts, Joel's prophecy (that "Your sons and daughters will prophesy"—2:17-18) is fulfilled in the declaration of what God has done in Jesus Christ (Acts 2:22-36). In 1 Corinthians 11, praying and prophesying are spoken about as two characteristic aspects of Christians in communal worship. Prayer is addressing the Lord; prophecy is addressing the word of the Lord to worshipers. In 1 Corinthians 14:29-33 the activity of Christian prophets is defined as addressing the content of divine revelation to the church for its instruction and encouragement. This purpose of prophetic speech is central in Paul's contrast of prophesying with speaking in tongues: strengthening, encouraging, comforting (14:3).

We may summarize the above distinctions as follows: Paul

understood "tongues" as inspired, ecstatic utterance which in
itself is unintelligible. Its native, proper place is the arena of
prayer (14:2, 16). He understands "prophesying" as inspired utterance of revelation (probably including both the gospel, that is,
God's act in Christ, and further revelation of God's purposes
based on that event), which is addressed to the church in intelligible speech for its continuing growth. With this background
and working definitions we are now ready to follow Paul's argument which surrounds our saying.

The larger context is provided by the chapters which precede
12—14, where Paul addresses problems in the church's corporate
life, specifically in the setting of worship. A primary and central
principle for Christian action is the principle of edification. All
Christian life and action is to be governed by the question: does
it benefit others? Does it lead to their salvation and/or growth
in faith? Is it for their good? (8:1, 9, 13; 9:12, 19-22; 10:23-24,
31-33; 11:21, 33). This principle continues as a guiding trajectory
in Paul's discussion of the place and function of spiritual gifts in
1 Corinthians 12—14.

The focus of that discussion is on the relative merits of
"tongues" and "prophesying" (in chapter 14). But Paul uses
"prophesying" in order to deal with what seems to be the core
of the issue in Corinth: a glorification of the gift of speaking in
tongues in such a way that the other gifts, as well as those who
possessed them, were minimized. Those who spoke in tongues
apparently saw this gift as a sign of their superior spirituality.
Such a view would naturally emerge among a faction of the
believers in Corinth who believed themselves to have been freed
from all responsible relationships and practical ethical concerns.
(See the discussion of the Corinthian "superspiritualists" in chapters 15—17 above.)

In the context of worship, these superspiritualists gloried in an
obviously inspired phenomenon as the ultimate validation that

they were free from earthbound existence, including rational, intelligible speech. Paul's question to them here, as earlier in connection with other problems, is: How does this gift contribute to the salvation or strengthening of others, rather than just the edification of the self (14:4)?

The foundations for tackling the issue are carefully laid in chapters 12—13. In summary, Paul's thought develops as follows. There are diverse gifts available for believers, but they all have their origin in God's Spirit (12:4-6). The implication is that no one has any ground for pride! The manifestation of this one Spirit in the diverse gifts is for the good of all (12:7). Thus, the possession of a particular gift is not for one's own benefit. It is the Spirit who determines how the gifts are distributed (12:11). Therefore, the possessor of one gift has no basis for feeling especially favored or in any sense elevated over one who does not have the same gift.

This series of thoughts is now buttressed by the picture of the church as the body of Christ, compared to the living organism of the human body (12:12-27). The main purpose is to affirm that, despite all the variety of persons and their gifts in the church, there should be no division; all parts should be concerned about all others (12:25).

Having stressed the *importance and validity* of all members of the body, and with them their diverse gifts, Paul now goes on to show that, with regard to the guiding principles of Christian life and action—namely, that others may be saved and built up—some callings and gifts take priority, are more foundational than others, and contribute more directly and substantially to that purpose.

Though he begins the list of callings and gifts by enumerating ("first apostles, second prophets, third teachers"—14:28), he does not continue that enumeration through the remaining list of gifts. The threefold ministry of the word—namely foundational apostolic witness to the gospel, prophetic proclamation of the gospel to the church, and instruction in the meaning and practical implications of the gospel—is clearly primary, while the other activities designated by the gifts (14:28) are dependent on, and secondary to, the "word" ministries. The fact that the gift of tongues is named last does not necessarily mean that it is "least" in a hierarchical order (since the five gifts are not numbered). It is more probable that Paul names it last because for the Corinthian enthusiasts it had top billing. It is, however, eminently clear that "tongues" belongs to a group of gifts which stand on a level below that of the ministries of the word. That is confirmed by Paul's summary sentence in 12:31, "But eagerly desire the greater gifts." It may be assumed from what follows in chapter 14 that prophetic proclamation (preaching) and teaching are those "greater gifts."

The injunction to desire the greater gifts is followed by a call to an even greater preoccupation, "And now I will show you the most excellent way" (12:31—"a still more excellent way," RSV). Even better than seeking the greater gifts, Paul argues, is following the way of love (13:1). For, as he so eloquently shows in chapter 13, both the lesser and the greater gifts will someday cease. But love is eternal. Paul may have introduced this magnificent call to love because he knew that love is purely other-directed and would be the motivating power for seeking those gifts that build up others. Thus "Follow the way of love and eagerly desire spiritual gifts, especially the gift of prophecy" (14:1).

The stage is now set for the specific discussion of the nature, function and relative merit of tongues and prophecy (in which our hard saying is located). "Tongues" is the language of the heart, addressed to God (14:2). "Prophecy" is God's word addressed to people for their encouragement and comfort (14:3). "Tongues" are primarily a private matter; they edify the self.

"Prophecy" is a public matter; it edifies the church (14:4).

Paul affirms the importance of both the personal and the public dimension of the contrasting gifts when he expresses his wish that they all had the gift of tongues, and then immediately qualifies that wish with his even greater wish: "but I would rather have you prophesy" (14:5). Private, ecstatic experience, especially in the intimacy of one's prayer relationship with God, is not to be rejected ("Do not forbid speaking in tongues"—14:39). Paul knows its value from personal experience (14:18). Even in the context of public worship, it can have a place if it is made intelligible through interpretation (14:5) so that others can be "edified" (14:16-17).

Since "tongues" is recognized as a gift of the Spirit and is at the disposal of the Spirit, Paul can say, "I wish you all had it." It would be an evidence that the Spirit was at work in them. And yet, his operative principle (the good of others) leads him unqualifiedly toward preference for prophetic proclamation: "But in the church I would rather speak five intelligible words to instruct others than ten thousand words in a tongue" (14:19).

This analysis leads to these concluding, summary observations: None of the spiritual gifts is an absolute; only the way of love is. Therefore, neither the possession nor the exercise of any of them is a mark of spiritual superiority. Believers are to be open to the Spirit's gifts and when they receive them to exercise them gratefully and humbly. Any earnest seeking for particular gifts ought to be guided by the desire to be involved in strengthening the church so that the whole people of God may truly be the divinely ordered alternative to the brokenness of human society.

CHAPTER 27

Silence in the Churches

As in all the congregations
of the saints,
women should remain silent
in the churches.
1 CORINTHIANS 14:33-34

S*everal acute problems are raised by 1 Corinthians 14:33-34 for the* Bible reader who seeks to be a faithful interpreter of the whole counsel of God revealed in Scripture as well as an obedient follower of Christ.

First, a series of questions is forced on us by the text itself and the words which follow it in verses 34-35: Does the New Testament as a whole show that women were routinely excluded from verbal participation in Christian worship? *Why* are they not allowed to speak? Which "Law" is referred to in verse 34? How are "submission" and "silence" related?

A second series of questions is raised by the relation between this hard saying and the immediate and wider biblical context. How can Paul say earlier in this epistle that women are to have a head covering on while praying and proclaiming the gospel (11:3-16) and now in the same letter forbid verbal participation? Further, how are we to take the apparent discrepancy between this blanket prohibition and the fact that there are numerous examples of women's active participation in the worship life of early Christianity?

A review of the material under the heading "The Context of the Biblical Texts" in the introduction to this book would be helpful as we begin to deal with these issues in this hard saying.

The text we are looking at is located at the conclusion of a lengthy section (chapters 11-14) in which Paul deals with problem situations in the context of worship. He has dealt with proper decorum of men and women while praying and prophesying (11:2-16); with irregularities at the Lord's Supper (11:17-34); and finally with the nature, function, use and abuse of spiritual gifts (12—14), with special consideration of the ecstatic phenomenon "speaking in tongues" and "prophecy" (14:1-25).

It is apparent in the immediately surrounding context (14:26-40) of our saying (14:33-34), that the elevation and glorification of ecstatic, unintelligible utterance by some faction in the congregation (see chapter 26 above) created disorder and confusion in worship. Thus in addressing those who speak in tongues (vv. 27-28), he calls for order: they should speak "one at a time." The utterances should be interpreted (vs. 27), since without interpretation it would confound the hearers and cause them to wonder whether there is madness here (14:23). Without an interpreter, "the speaker should keep quiet in the church" (14:28). In addressing those who have the gift for prophetic proclamation of the gospel (14:29-33), the concern for order in worship is also evident. Their speaking is to be "in turn," that is, not all at the same time. The purpose of all verbal communication is "the strengthening of the church" (14:26) through the instruction and encouragement of everyone (14:31). That purpose, as Paul sees it, can only be accomplished when there is order in worship, "for God is not a God of disorder, but of peace" (14:33; see also 14:40).

All of the above shows that Paul is dealing with abuses and actions in worship which disrupt God's purposes and which therefore need correction. Within such a setting, our text seems clearly to belong to the category of "corrective texts" whose purpose is focused toward a local situation. Paul's word that "women should remain silent in the churches" would therefore seem, at least primarily, to have authoritative import ("What I am writing to you is the Lord's command"—14:37) for the particular situation in Corinth (as well as similar situations; for example, the one addressed in 1 Tim 2:11-12). One must be careful therefore not to jump to the conclusion immediately that Paul's injunction has implications for all women in all churches.

Support for restraint in this area comes from both other things Paul writes and practices in the early churches which show that women's vocal participation in worship and in other instructional or leadership roles was accepted and affirmed. Paul himself acknowledges in this same letter the validity and appropriateness of women as full participants in public prayer and the proclamation of the gospel (11:5, 13). What he finds invalid and unacceptable is that they engage in this activity without a head covering, since that rejection of cultural/religious custom creates a potential stumbling block. Paul even affirms in that context that "the churches of God" recognize no other practice (11:16), namely, the appropriateness of a head covering for women who are praying and prophesying in the church.

If Paul believed that women should be silent in the churches in a comprehensive, universal sense, he would not have spent so much time (in chapter 11) instructing women what to do with their heads; he would have simply forbidden their practice of praying and prophesying in the assembled congregation. (Note: Other New Testament texts which bear on the role of women in the early church will be discussed in relation to the hard saying in 1 Timothy 2:11-12.)

Paul's larger view—which acknowledged and validated the vocal participation of women in the churches—is supported in other New Testament writings. Thus the proclamation of the "wonders of God" (namely, his redemptive work in and through Jesus of Nazareth—Acts 2:11, 22-36) is interpreted in Peter's Pentecost sermon as the fulfillment of the prophecy of Joel 2:28-29 that in the last days, under the inspiration of God's outpoured Spirit, "Your sons and daughters will prophesy. . . . Even on my servants, *both men and women*, I will pour out my Spirit in those days, and they will prophesy" (Acts 2:17-18, emphasis mine). In keeping with this prophetic word and the commencement of its fulfillment at Pentecost, Luke mentions matter-of-factly that the evangelist Philip had four daughters who were engaged in the prophetic ministry of the good news (Acts 21:8-9)

In light of this evidence that women in the early churches were moved by the Spirit to engage in ministries of the Word side by side with men, it is difficult, if not impossible, to understand Paul's injunction as a categorical imperative intended for all churches in all places in all times. Rather, the injunction must be understood within its own context (and for similar contexts "in all the congregations of the saints"—14:33), as addressing a problem in Corinth which needed correcting.

We have already seen above that the particular problem was disorder, lack of regularity, and confusion in public worship. This situation was apparently caused by the inappropriate expression of both the gift of prophecy and speaking in tongues (14:26-31). It is thus probable that the admonition to silence is in some way related to women's participation in the inappropriate use of these gifts. It is possible that women in the Corinthian congregation, due to the liberating experience of the gospel from all sorts of cultural and religious bondage, may have been at the forefront of noninterpreted, unintelligible utterance (*glossolalia*) and enthusiastic prophetic proclamation which did not yield the "congregational floor" to others. Some may have continued to speak at the same time another was prophesying, creating noisy confusion in which no one could be "instructed and encouraged."

That such a connection existed between the women who are asked to be silent and the disorderly expression of tongues and prophetic speech receives support from two sets of parallel phrases in our texts. In addressing those speaking in tongues without the benefit of interpretation, Paul says, "the speaker *should keep quiet in the church*" (14:28). Then, in 14:34, he uses the exact same words: "the women *should keep quiet in the churches*." The NIV variation in translation does not reflect the fact that the Greek verb (*sigaō*) is the same in both.

Second, in addressing the issues of disorderly prophetic speaking (14:29-32), Paul again urges silence on some so that others can speak. The NIV's "the first speaker should stop" (14:30) again does not reflect the fact that the verb *sigaō* ("remain silent") is also used here. But more important, in calling on the prophets in the congregation to recognize that they are mutually accountable to each other, Paul says, "The spirits of prophets are subject to the control of prophets" (14:32). The Greek word rendered "subject to the control of" is *hypotassō*. That is the same word Paul uses in 14:34, where he follows the admonition to silence (according to the NIV) with the words, "[they] must be in submission." In other words, prophets must be in submission to other prophets (and thus to each other) in the church.

If, as seems likely, women were prominently in that group of prophets who were disposed to be "disorderly," Paul may, in 14:34, be addressing them specifically with regard to this matter of submission to other prophets for the sake of order and peace

(14:32-33). These parallelisms in the imperatives to "keep quiet" and "to be in submission" strongly suggest that the problem of disorderly participation in prophetic proclamation and tongues was particularly prominent among women believers in Corinth, and that it is with respect to this context that Paul's admonitions must be understood.

A final problem needs brief attention. What is the "Law" on which the injunction to submission is based (14:34)? Assuming that the submission envisioned is to the men/husbands in the congregation, some have sought Old Testament texts which would ground such an injunction. The most common text cited from "the Law" is Genesis 3:16. Two factors militate against it. Wherever Paul deals with the relation between men and women, he never appeals to this passage. Further, it is clear from the context of Genesis 2—3 that 3:16—"Your desire will be for your husband, and he will rule over you"—does not announce God's created design for "male leadership," but is the statement of a cursed existence because of sin. Surely Paul knew that Christ's redemptive work freed human beings from the curse of Eden.

Others see in Paul's term ("as the Law says") a reference to both Jewish and Gentile norms which restricted women's public participation, and these restrictions existed within the context of male-dominant cultures. Yet Paul uses the word "be submissive" without saying "to whom." Thus the assumption that it is to men/husbands may not be warranted. It is more likely that he is referring back to the statement that "prophets are to be submissive to (other) prophets" (14:32). The questions "submissive to whom or what?" would then have an answer in the immediate context: either other prophets, or to the principle of order which has its origin in God (14:33).

Paul's operative principle for congregational life and worship is constant. Whatever hinders the movement of the gospel, causes confusion rather than growth, offends rather than encourages or strengthens, builds up the self at the expense of others—all this is contrary to God's intention. And insofar as the women in Corinth and elsewhere in the young churches used their gifts contrary to God's intention, the injunction to silence is an appropriate, authoritative word. The principle which underlies the injunction is authoritative for both men and women in all churches.

• C H A P T E R 2 8 •

Baptism
for the
Dead

Now if there is no resurrection,
what will those do who are baptized
for the dead? If the dead are
not raised at all, why are people
baptized for them?
1 CORINTHIANS 15:29

From the rather straightforward way in which Paul discusses baptism for the dead, it appears that both for him and for his readers the rite or practice of "being baptized for [literally, 'on behalf of'] the dead" was as obvious and clear as it is puzzling and obscure for us. What is Paul's point in referring to such a practice? What is the meaning and purpose of the practice? Did Paul approve or disapprove it?

First a word about the context in which this text appears. In chapter 15, Paul gives an elaborate apologetic for both the resurrection of Christ and the future resurrection of the dead. This apologetic assumes that among the Corinthian Christians were some who denied the very concept of resurrection. Such a denial seems to have emerged out of a view of reality which rejected the goodness of physical life and held that only the human spirit or soul (the immaterial aspect) was the object of redemption. Thus among the superspiritualists in Corinth there were the "libertines" for whom concrete, bodily realities, including sexual relations, had no ultimate significance; for them, anything was possible. (See the discussion of the results of such a view in chapters 15-17.) Paul's discussion of the resurrection responds to questions raised in the congregation by the views of these hyperspiritualists.

Paul's apologetic is expressed in a series of "if/then" arguments: If there is no resurrection, then Christ has not been raised (15:13). If Christ has not been raised, then our preaching and your faith are futile (15:14, 17) and those Christians who have already died are lost (15:18). If the dead are not raised, then "let us eat and drink, for tomorrow we die" and that's the end of it (15:32).

Our text is part of this series of arguments. Though the Greek of the first part of verse 29 does not contain the phrase "no resurrection" (as in NIV; compare NASB, RSV), the preposition *epei* ("now if" or "otherwise") clearly carries this sense from the previous "if/then" series, as well as from the latter part of verse 29, "If the dead are not raised, why then . . . ?"

Apart from the question of the nature and meaning of the practice and Paul's attitude toward it, the force of the argument is unambiguous: If there is no resurrection, if the dead are not raised, what is the point of the rite in which people are baptized on their behalf? Will not those who undergo this ritual look like fools if in fact there is no resurrection? No matter what efficacy is believed to come from such vicarious baptism, the whole enterprise is a total waste of effort and time! The core of this apologetic is of course the contradiction between their belief and their practice. They believe that there is no resurrection; yet their practice belies that belief.

What was the practice and its purpose? The reference to baptism on behalf of the dead in 15:29 is unique in the New Testament. Its mention here indicates that it was practiced by some Christians in Corinth (if not generally by the congregation as a whole). Its absence from the rest of the New Testament, as well as the apostolic fathers probably indicates that it was not a common practice. Practices with some affinity to it show up in some second- and third-century heretical groups and may be developments from the practice mentioned by Paul. But these later practices are of no help in determining what the Corinthian believers intended in this ritual.

The scantiness of the evidence has given rise to scores of interpretations, some of which are fanciful and highly speculative (for example, that it was a practice of being baptized on the tombs of the dead). However, the plain reading of the text probably allows for no more than two possibilities: (1) some Christians in Corinth (presumably persons who had already undergone their own baptism) were undergoing the rite on behalf of dead relatives or friends; (2) the rite was being practiced on behalf of persons who were Christians, but who had died before baptism was administered. This latter possibility would certainly fit a time in the history of the church when those who professed faith in Christ went through an extended "probationary" period of as much as a year before they were baptized and became full members of the Christian fellowship.

Baptism on their behalf would be a visible demonstration that these departed had appropriated Christ's atoning death and, therefore, would be raised by God. What argues against this second possibility is the New Testament evidence that in the early decades, baptism was generally administered almost immediately after persons came to faith in Christ (for example, Acts

2:37-41; 8:34-38; 10:44-48; 16:29-33). Yet it is quite possible that even in this early period, due to circumstances or illness or large-scale epidemics, numerous believers died before baptism had been administered.

As to the meaning and purpose of the practice, the wording suggests some "vicarious" significance. Those who underwent the rite "on behalf of" a deceased person must have held to a belief that by this act their resurrection could be secured. If the second view mentioned above is adopted, baptism on behalf of dead—but unbaptized—believers, could have been understood as a visible sign and celebration that these departed ones had appropriated Christ's atoning death for themselves in faith and would therefore participate in the resurrection. In this sense, the practice would certainly not have violated Paul's own understanding of the significance of baptism, and he would probably not have rejected the practice. According to Romans 6, baptism was for Paul a dramatic re-enactment of death and resurrection: first of all, death to sin and resurrection to new life, but also participation, by faith, in Christ's death and resurrection; and finally, a powerful proclamation of victory over death in the final resurrection.

If, however, this vicarious baptism was on behalf of nonbelievers, then a view of the nature and efficacy of baptism beyond Paul's own view must have been held by these Christians. Such a view (some would call it highly sacramental; others magical) would have understood the baptismal ritual as so effective that its benefits would accrue to the one for whom it was enacted. The departed person would have been seen to be included in the sphere of the saving faith of those who enacted the ritual.

Underlying such a view, and leading to it, is no doubt a deep concern, present among believers from the beginning, about all those who died before the event of Christ in history. Were those who died before the Incarnation, or those who died before the gospel was preached in their communities, deprived of the opportunity to be redeemed and join the community of the resurrected ones? The practice of baptism on behalf of the dead may have been an early response to such concerns. That same concern also lies behind the idea that Christ entered the realm of the dead after his death and before his resurrection in order to offer salvation to all those who died before the Incarnation (1 Peter 3:18-20).

CHAPTER 29

A Veil over Their Minds

*But their minds were made dull,
for to this day the same
veil remains when the
old covenant is read.*
2 CORINTHIANS 3:14

These words are written by Paul about his own people Israel who, in respect to a knowledge of God and his purposes, have been and continue to be in a twilight zone. The questions raised by this statement are, Why is that so? How were their minds made dull? Who or what caused this? What is the veil which covers them when the Law is read?

This text is part of a section in which Paul contrasts the old covenant and its results with the new covenant and its results. The old covenant—though that was not its intention—leads to death (3:6, 9), as the history of Israel's disobedience and her rejection of the Messiah clearly demonstrates for Paul.

The new covenant, inaugurated in Christ, leads to life (3:6, 9), as Paul's experience and his understanding of the Incarnation also clearly demonstrates. Behind this contrast stands Paul's deep conviction that the old covenant, focused in the giving of the Law, reveals the nature and purposes of God indirectly (Gal 3:19-20), while the new covenant, focused in Christ, reveals God directly and fully. Christ is the very image of God (2 Cor 4:4); he is the incarnation of God's "fullness" (Col 1:19; 2:9).

Within the context of this overall view, Paul's discussion, which leads to this text, develops as follows. He sees his ministry of proclaiming the gospel as resulting in a new covenant community in which the revelation of God is not present on inscribed tablets but engraved on hearts by the Spirit of God (3:3-6). In the use of this imagery, Paul is clearly reflecting the prophecy of Jeremiah 31:31-34 about the promise of a new covenant where the will of God will be written on people's hearts. Paul understands the church as the fulfillment of this prophetic vision. The contrast between "indirect" and "direct" contact with the living God is here implicitly given.

Paul continues the contrast by reflecting on the experience of Moses and Israel when the Ten Commandments were given. According to Exodus 34:29-35, when Moses brought the tablets from Mt. Sinai, his face was radiant because he had been in the presence of the glory of the Lord (see Ex 33:18, 22), and the people were afraid to come near. Then Moses would veil his face, thus covering the reflection of God's glory in his face. Paul contrasts this indirect and muted mediation and reflection of God's glory at the time of the establishing of the old covenant with the greater glory of the new covenant, established by the presence of the Spirit (3:7-11). That Spirit is the "Spirit of the Lord" (3:17), and it is that Lord in whose face "the light of the knowledge of the glory of God" is revealed fully (4:6).

Having established this contrast, Paul now uses the veil—

which covered Moses' face to cover the reflected radiance of
God's glory (3:13)—to *symbolize* Israel's past and present blindness
"when the old covenant is read" (3:14).

Paul knew, on the basis of the history of his people and his
own experience, that the words of Scripture with regard to Israel's "dullness of mind" (3:14) and blindness of sight are true.
What causes this lack of full comprehension and unobstructed
vision?

According to Deuteronomy 29, in the context of a covenant
renewal ceremony, Moses tells the people that even though they
have seen and experienced the mighty deeds of the Lord on their
behalf, they have not really grasped its full significance, for "to
this day the LORD has not given you a mind that understands or
eyes that see or ears that hear" (29:4). The context shows that
Israel's breaking of God's covenant with them stands in the background. With their own eyes and ears and minds they failed to
grasp God's truth for them. The statement "the LORD has not
given you . . ." does not mean that the Lord caused their disobedience, but rather that if their eyes and ears and minds were
really in tune with the Lord, the mighty works of God on their
behalf would have been seen for what they were—namely, evidences of God's steadfast love and faithfulness (Ex 34:6). By not
"giving them minds that understand," God allowed their minds
to dull.

That same mysterious relation between human decision and
divine action is expressed in the context of the prophet Isaiah's
call, where he is told that the word of the Lord which he will
address to the people of Israel will make their heart calloused,
their ears dull and their eyes closed (Is 6:10). This is a prophetic
anticipation of what in fact happened as a result of Isaiah's
preaching: the nation continued on its way of disobedience toward national collapse and exile. Because this was the result of
the word of the Lord which Isaiah proclaimed, it could be said

that the Lord "closed their eyes." What is reflected here is the lack of precise distinction in Hebraic thought between primary and secondary causes. Since God is sovereign, human will and freedom to decide for or against God were often subsumed under divine sovereignty.

An increasing sense of individual and corporate responsibility before God is reflected in the Greek translation of the Hebrew Scriptures. There the Hebrew of Isaiah 6:10—"Make the heart of this people calloused . . ."—is rendered, "This people's heart has become calloused, they hardly hear with their ears, and they have closed their eyes." The translators understood the Isaiah passage to mean that Israel's disobedience led to their lack of understanding.

It is this background in the Old Testament which is reflected in Paul's statement "their minds were made dull." And the rejection of the Messiah shows that "to this day" their rebellion against God continues. That is the veil which remains. Whenever "Moses is read" (that is the law—3:15), the veil remains. For, as Paul shows elsewhere, the Law was only able to reveal human sin; it could not save (Romans 3:20). But, when one turns to the Lord, so Paul concludes, the veil is taken away (3:15).

That conclusion surely emerged from Paul's own experience. In the very attempt to obey the Law, he found himself opposing the true purposes of God. In Christ, those true purposes have been revealed; not indirectly, but directly. Therefore, we can "reflect the Lord's glory" (3:18). The veil of disobedience and dullness has been removed.

· C H A P T E R 3 0 ·

All the Old Has Gone?

If anyone is in Christ,
he is a new creation;
the old has gone,
the new has come!
2 CORINTHIANS 5:17

Paul's *joyful proclamation in 2 Corinthians 5:17 expresses a conviction* which seems all too frequently contradicted by our experience. We affirm that life in Christ produces a new kind of living and are embarrassed to find so little difference between our actual living and the lives of those who make no such claims. We rejoice in the forgiveness of God for our sinfulness and then recognize how our living often fails to convey this reality to others. We worship the Christ who gave his life for others, yet devote so much time and energy to promote ourselves. We proclaim allegiance to Christ as Lord while living by priorities and values which indicate that there are indeed "many gods and lords" by which we really live.

Like us, the early Christians to whom Paul addressed those words recognized that in many ways the "old" remained with them and the "new" life of faith in Christ needed to be appropriated again and again. These early Christians saw that Rome and its oppressive power continued. Injustice and immorality prevailed in their world. They experienced continuing bondage in their personal lives, bitter strife within communal Christian life, the continuing reality of personal failure, anxiety, frustration and sin. Why the old when the new is come? Why are these things still with us, if it is true that "the old has gone" and "the new has come"?

How are we to understand this tension between Christian affirmation and Christian experience? There have been two main ways by which Christians have sought to deal with this problem. Both ways have arisen out of an understanding of human nature which sees us as consisting of essentially two parts: the physical (flesh) and the spiritual (soul), which are opposed to each other.

One way manifested itself as early as A.D. 50 in the Christian community at Corinth. It was the "spiritualizing" of Christian faith. The argument went something like this: "Since the body, the flesh, the physical aspect is at best weak, at worst corrupt, what we need to do is to concentrate on the spiritual side, on the soul. And since, through Christ, our souls have been redeemed, it really does not matter what we do with our bodies." It does not take much imagination to see where this way of splitting the human personality leads. In Corinth, it led to *libertinism*, which manifested itself in a complete disregard for the moral-ethical life and a haughty disdain for the brother or sister who had not attained to such a "liberated spirituality."

A second response to such a dualistic view of human nature manifested itself during Paul's missionary activity in Asia Minor.

It was the *legalizing* of the Christian faith. The argument here
went as follows: "The flesh really interferes with the attempt of
the human spirit to be in perfect communion with God. Therefore, 'the flesh,' with all its passions and desires, must be made
subservient to the spirit. We must impose—by means of codes
of conduct—such close strictures on our lives that the inner pu-
rity of the spirit is not somehow defiled by the flesh." The extreme form of this response was a rigorous asceticism and monastic isolation from entanglements with the world.

Much of contemporary Christian thinking continues to be influenced by such dualism. Sometimes it becomes an escape hatch
from the demands of Christian discipleship. At other times it
forms the basis of a disregard for bodily, concrete things and an
elevation of the spiritual or a suppression of the physical with a
view to the purification of the soul.

If the above ways of dealing with the basic tension in Christian
existence are inadequate, how then are we to understand the
presence of that tension, how are we to account for it, and how
are we to come to grips with it?

There were Greek thinkers, prior to and contemporary with
the birth of Christianity, who saw the human body as the pris-
onhouse or tomb of the soul. They believed that salvation con-
sisted of the liberation of a person's higher self, the spirit or soul,
from its entrapment with the body. This understanding of human nature, which has influenced much Christian thought, must
be decidedly rejected as contrary to the biblical point of view. In
the witness of the Bible, the *total being* is the object of God's
redemptive purposes. As physical-spiritual beings we are the objects of God's forgiving act in Christ. In our *wholeness* we stand
under the constraining love of Christ by which we become new
creations. In our concrete existence we can be transformed into
the image of Christ. The human person—in the context of relationship to others—is the locus of God's intervention. To af-

firm less than that is to limit God!

If a dividing of the human personality into antagonistic physical and spiritual components cannot account for the tension between the "old" and the "new," what can? What, we must ask, is Paul expressing in our text? In what sense are Christians "new creations"?

An instructive perspective comes to light when Paul's word is seen against the backdrop of Israel's prophetic hope. One of the main features of that hope was the belief that the *end of time* was going to be like the *beginning of time*. When the prophets spoke about the expectation of God's final coming and reign in human history, they frequently described that time in imagery associated in the Old Testament with paradise and the original creation. A new creation was going to replace the fallen old creation. Isaiah's picture of the return of paradise is a striking example of this prophetic expectation: "The wolf will live with the lamb, the leopard will lie down with the goat, the calf and the lion and the yearling together; and a little child will lead them" (Is 11:6).

Now, for Paul, the end of time had dawned on a broken world. The end of the ages had broken into the old age (see 1 Cor 10:11). The world was a new world insofar as it had encountered the Creator in the Christ. The person "in Christ" was part of a new humanity, created in Christ Jesus for a new existence. As Adam and Eve, the typical representative human beings, stood before the Creator in radical freedom, so the new person in Christ stands before the Creator in radical freedom. In some sense, the situation before the Fall has been re-created for the Christian. In that sense the Christian is a "new creation." As Adam and Eve were faced with the decision to give allegiance to God the Creator or to create their own gods and give allegiance to them (see Rom 1:20-23), so the new-creation person has been freed from the Fall's bondage for the same decision. As they lived with the possibility of either dependence on the Creator or independence from him, so the new-creation person exists within that possibility. As they could either exist in fellowship with their Maker or hide from God among the trees, so the new-creation person can live in trust before God or make jungles in which to hide from God.

God's redeeming love in Christ has reclaimed us for relationship with our Creator. In this relationship we are free from the *bondage to sin* which characterized us while alienated from God. But this relationship *does not automatically remove us* from the influence of sin's reality which surrounds us in all arenas of life.

For Paul, "the old" which has gone is the condition of alienation from God and its bondage to sin. "The new" which has come is our relationship with God in Christ, a relationship which empowers us for a kind of living in which the continuing reality of sin can be overcome again and again. To be a "new creation" is not to be perfect or faultless, or immune from anger and pain, or insulated from the tough experiences of life. Rather, to be a "new creation" is to live life turned toward the God whose grace has reclaimed us in Christ.

· C H A P T E R 3 1 ·

Yoked
with
Unbelievers

*Do not be yoked together
with unbelievers.*
2 CORINTHIANS 6:14

There are two ways in which 2 Corinthians 6:14 may be viewed as a hard saying. It may be hard because we don't like the rigorous implications it seems to have for our everyday relationships with persons who are not believers. If it is hard for this reason it should not be made easier, for that would be to obscure its meaning. The saying may, however, be hard because (1) it seems to present the incompatibility between believer and unbeliever more narrowly than other New Testament texts, and (2) it is not clear what being "yoked together" means precisely and how it is to be put into practice. A careful look at the text and its context should help.

One of the major themes in 2 Corinthians is the defense of the integrity of Paul's apostolic ministry, the authenticity of the gospel which he preached and the implications that gospel had for the life of Christians. It is clear from statements in both canonical letters that Paul's relationship with Corinth was a tumultuous one, giving rise to several visits and as many as four letters. There were elements in the church who opposed Paul and his teachings, and because of that opposition (often arising out of misunderstandings of what Paul had said or written earlier), the church at Corinth was in danger of self-destructing again and again.

In our discussion of 2 Corinthians 5:17 (chapter 30 above) we saw that central to Paul's thought was the conviction that "in Christ" believers were "new creatures," their old allegiances had been replaced by a new relationship with God, "who reconciled us to himself" (5:17-18). On the basis of that truth, Paul knew that God had called him into the "ministry of reconciliation." Recognizing that reconciliation in the divine-human relationship had far-reaching implications for human relationships, Paul was grieved by those who opposed him and the gospel (2 Cor 2:1-4) and was concerned about their salvation. So he pleads earnestly with them: "We implore you on Christ's behalf: Be reconciled to God" (5:20) and "We urge you not to receive the grace of God in vain" (6:1).

From his earlier letter (1 Cor) it is clear that there were several areas in their life as a congregation and as individual believers where God's grace seemed to be in vain (for example, continuing participation in pagan cultic rituals, 1 Cor 6; 10; taking disagreements into pagan courts, 1 Cor 6). How can "receiving God's grace in vain" be avoided? Our verse is a response to that question.

The Greek word for "yoked together" is found only here in the New Testament. In the Greek Old Testament, the word is used in the prohibition against breeding cattle with a different species of animal (Lev 19:19). From this use of the Greek word comes the meaning "mismating," which several translations employ for our text (RSV; NEB, "Do not unite yourselves with unbelievers; they are no fit mates for you"). From this rendering of the word has emerged what is probably the commonest understanding of 6:14; namely, that Paul warns against marriage between believers and nonbelievers.

Though this understanding may be a valid application of the idea, the context of the passage suggests that marriage was not what Paul had in mind here. He seems to use the term in its more general meaning of "unevenly yoked," such as placing animals of a different species in the same harness. Paul may have used the prohibition against such yoking in Deuteronomy 22:10 as a metaphor[1]: there is a decided difference between the Christian and the non-Christian. There is a basic incompatibility which must be recognized and which has implications for life in an environment of unbelief. What is the nature of that incompatibility? And what are its implications?

The statement "Do not be yoked together with unbelievers" is followed by a series of five antithetical questions which define the nature of incompatibility between believers and unbelievers. The questions are rhetorical; thus the answers are obvious. What do righteousness and wickedness, light and darkness, Christ and Belial,[2] believer and unbeliever, the temple of God and idols, have in common (vv. 14-16)? Absolutely nothing! "For we are the temple of the living God" (v. 16).

The idea of Christians being, collectively, the temple of God was already laid before the Corinthians in Paul's earlier epistle (1 Cor 3:16). There they were also reminded that God's temple was sacred (holy), and they were that temple (3:17). They were to "flee from sexual immortality" (6:18) and "from idolatry" (10:14), for all forms of wickedness are incompatible with the kingdom of God (6:9-10). In 2 Corinthians 6:14-18 the reminder that they are God's temple (6:16) is followed, via a series of Old Testament texts, by the call to really be God's holy people among whom he is present as in a temple. This exploration of the temple imagery as applied to the Christian community in the world closes with a final exhortation: "Let us purify ourselves from everything which contaminates body and spirit, perfecting holiness out of reverence for God" (7:1).

The whole passage from 6:14 on seems to drive toward this climax. Here is the key to what "not being yoked with unbelievers" means. It means that the Christian is in process, moving toward holiness. The concept of holiness, as applied to both the temple and the people of God, is grounded in the Old Testament. The Hebrew word, meaning "separated," always has a double meaning: *separated from* evil and *dedicated to* the service of God. Separation from evil is demonstrated by a distinctive way of life which evidences moral behavior of the highest order. Dedication to God's service is demonstrated by the rejection of all idolatrous contamination (1 Cor 10:14; 2 Cor 6:16), whether in its ancient or modern forms (for "idolatry" is giving ultimate allegiance to beings or powers or things or values, rather than to God).

What are the implications for today? Not monastic isolation from the world. In 1 Corinthians 5:10 he recognizes that disassociation from immoral, worldly persons is impossible, since that would mean that one "would have to leave this world" (see also Jesus' prayer in Jn 17:15, "not that you take them out of the world but that you protect them from the evil one"). In 1 Corinthians 7:12-16, he recognizes that the marriage of a believer and unbeliever may lead to the sanctification of the unbelieving spouse. And in 1 Corinthians 10:27, he recognizes the possibility of believers at dinner parties in the homes of unbelieving friends or neighbors.

Separatist movements in church history, in the attempt to be faithful to the radical nature of Paul's call for holiness, have often interpreted that call in terms of external associations or contacts or affiliations. Such a focus has often missed what seems to be the core of Paul's concern; namely, that while living in the world and in contact with unbelievers, Christians have nothing in common with the darkness and evil and unrighteousness and immorality that claims the loyalties of those who are as yet not reconciled with God.

Thus to be "yoked with unbelievers" is to be of one heart and mind with them, co-opted by the values that guide them, seduced by their commitments to various "gods and lords" (1 Cor 8:5), conformed to a view of things which dismisses absolute truth and moral absolutes. Christians, according to Paul, are new creations living in the midst of the old order. As such, they are to "live as children of light," bearing "the fruit of the light" which is "goodness, righteousness and truth" (Eph 5:8-9).

Notes

[1]In light of the fact that both Leviticus 19:19 and Deuteronomy 22:9-10 forbid various unequal combinations, such as sowing different seeds in the same soil, garments made from different materials, it is apparent that the metaphor "unevenly yoked" speaks of incompatibility, such as our common expression "oil and water don't mix."

[2]Paul uses the name *Belial* only here as the opponent of Christ; his usual term is Satan. Belial (or Beliar; the spellings vary) is the name given to the head of evil forces opposed to God in the noncanonical literature of Judaism (for example, Jubilees 1:20; 15:33; Martyrdom of Isaiah 1:9; 2:4; 3:11).

• C H A P T E R   3 2 •

Condemning Opponents

If anybody is preaching
to you a gospel other than what
you accepted, let him
be eternally condemned!
GALATIANS 1:9

P aul's curse in Galatians 1:9 is a hard saying for two reasons: it does not seem to be in agreement with some other statements of Paul; it seems diametrically opposed to the teaching of Jesus with regard to our attitudes and actions toward those who are opposed to us.

In Romans 2:1-4 Paul lays down the principle that judgment passed on others, is in some sense "reflexive," that is, when we pass judgment on others, we condemn ourselves at the same time. For only God knows the truth about us, and only he is able therefore to pass judgment. We are mere creatures, both limited with respect to the truth about others and the truth about ourselves. We, like all others, are sinners (Rom 3:23); that is the ultimate reason we ought not to pass judgment.

This same sentiment is expressed again in a context where there is mutual judging going on within the congregation (Rom 14:1-13). Here the admonition not to judge others in respect to certain practices and beliefs considered inappropriate or wrong is based on the assertion that each disciple is accountable ultimately to the Lord (14:4), and all will equally "stand before God's judgment seat" (14:10). The larger perspective which ought to guide Christians' attitudes toward opponents is derived by Paul from the teaching of Jesus. Thus, echoing Matthew 5:44, Paul says, "Bless those who persecute you; bless and do not curse" (Rom 12:14). Our task as Christians is to "overcome evil with good" (Rom 12:21).

The overall teaching, attitude and life of Jesus stand also in apparent conflict with Paul's word of condemnation. Jesus' radical imperative on the matter is: "Do not judge, or you too will be judged. For in the same way you judge others, you will be judged" (Mt 7:1-2). The reason given for this imperative is that our own vision may be so impaired that it is sheer hypocrisy to try to remove the sawdust particle in the other's eye (7:3, 5). The proper response to those who are opposed to us is to love them and pray for them (Mt 5:44). Beyond these words, Jesus' entire life is a demonstration of his words' validity. He did not come into a world opposed to God to condemn it but to save it (Jn 3:17). Because of his deep compassion he weeps over Jerusalem (Lk 19:41), the city that kills the prophets and those (like Jesus) sent to her (Lk 13:34). To the adulteress he speaks the word of forgiveness rather than judgment (Jn 8:10-11); to the criminal hanging on a cross next to him he speaks the word of grace (Lk 23:39-43).

As Paul's words against judging seem to stand in conflict with his harsh words in Galatians 1:9, so the larger picture of Jesus' teaching and life, characterized by love and compassion, by humility and forgiveness, stands in apparent conflict with another dimension. Thus Jesus' words and actions could be uncompromisingly harsh toward those who opposed him and his ministry and whose "piety" excluded the redemptive work of God. He calls the religious leaders of his own people "sons of the devil," whose desire they carry out (Jn 8:44). Those who oppose his ministry of releasing the possessed from bondage are called "an evil generation" (Lk 11:29), who will be judged and condemned (Lk 11:31-32). Those who oppose the work of the Spirit of God in and through his life (Mt 12:28) will be condemned eternally; for them there is no forgiveness (Mt 12:31-32). Words of bitter denunciation are spoken against the teachers of the law and Pharisees, whom he calls "children of hell" (Mt 23:15), "blind fools" (Mt 23:17), "whitewashed tombs" (Mt 23:27), "snakes" and a "brood of vipers" who cannot "escape being condemned to hell" (Mt 23:33).

When we carefully compare this radically harsh tone in Jesus' teaching with that strand in his life which exudes compassion and forgiveness, we recognize where the essential difference lies. He came as the incarnation of God's redemptive love, and wherever there is openness to it, forgiveness is given, grace is experienced, sin is overcome. But where there is absolute rejection of that redemptive love, where the work of God is identified as demonic, where truth is trampled under foot, there condemnation is pronounced. It is within this latter context of the rejection of God's redemptive love that our hard saying must be understood.

In Paul's epistle to the Galatians, the central issue addressed is this: the core of the gospel which Paul had preached and on which their faith was based is that we are justified, brought into right relationship with God solely by his grace and through faith, not by gaining a standing before God on the basis of obedience to the law (Gal 2:15-21). That gospel was being challenged by the so-called Judaizers; namely, Jewish Christians who demanded that gentile Christians observe the Mosaic law, including ritual observances such as special days, kosher foods and circumcision (3:1-7, 4:8-11, 17, 21-22). Those who respond to their teaching, who are led away from the truth (5:7), who now seek "to be justified by law, have been alienated from Christ" and have "fallen away from grace" (5:4).

For Paul the conflict between the gospel which he preached and the teaching of the Judaizers is a life-and-death struggle. Why? Because legalistic obedience, life before God based on religious achievement, does not bring into right relationship with God (2:16; 3:3); because that kind of life leads not to life-giving relationship with God, but to alienation from him (5:4), to rejection of God's grace (2:21), to a life of legalistic bondage (4:9, 21; 5:1), to the curse of death (3:10-13).

Those who teach this way are "false brothers" (2:4) who oppose the "truth of the gospel" (2:5, 14), confuse the believers (1:7), "pervert the gospel of Christ" (1:7), bewitch the saints (3:1). Therefore, let anyone who does this "be eternally condemned" (1:8-9). This strong language shows how serious the matter was for Paul. George Duncan puts it well when he calls these words "an imprecation such as we cannot imagine him using had it been merely his personal prestige . . . anything, in fact, but the gospel of Christ which was at stake."[1]

It is clear then that Paul is not calling for the condemnation of his opponents (that is, the Judaizers) because they are opposed *to him*, but rather because they are *enemies of the gospel*. That gospel is of divine origin, not of Paul's invention (1:11-12). Therefore, those who pervert it subvert God's redemptive purpose. On those who thus act and teach, the judgment of God is justly pronounced. Thus there is here no real conflict between Paul's general call for a nonjudgmental spirit and his strong word of judgment here, just as there is no real conflict between Jesus' teaching on love for one's opponents and his words of judgment. In both cases, where the work and truth of God is at stake, those who reject it stand under judgment.

Note

[1]George S. Duncan, *The Epistle of Paul to the Galatians* (London: Hodder and Stoughton, 1934), pp. 18-19.

CHAPTER 33

Christ of No Value

*I, Paul, tell you that
if you let yourselves be circumcised,
Christ will be of no value
to you at all.*
GALATIANS 5:2

Galatians 5:2 *seems to express a limitation in the work of Christ.*
Doesn't this verse devalue the extent and efficacy of Christ's life
and death? Can the submission to something as external as the
rite of circumcision blunt the effectiveness of his sacrificial
death?

The central theme of Galatians is that salvation is by faith and
not by works; that justification (that is, right relationship with
God) is the result of the gracious gift of God's Son, not human
achievement; that freedom from the bondage to sin does not
come by even the most meticulous obedience to the law, but
through the atoning death of Christ on the cross. This gospel

was being undermined and perverted by the so-called Judaizers.

These Jewish Christians opposed the Pauline gospel as antinomian ("against law"), apparently believing that in addition to God's work in Christ, both Jewish and Gentile Christians needed to observe the law, including particularly ceremonial and cultic observances, such as special days, kosher foods and circumcision (3:1-7; 4:8-11, 17, 21-22). Paul calls them the "circumcision group" (2:12), because their demand for obedience to the Mosaic law from the followers of the Messiah expressed itself most specifically and radically in the demand that Gentiles, in order to become full members in the new covenant community, be circumcised (6:12).

That demand of the Judaizers Paul rejects uncompromisingly (see chapter 32 above), because it sets up a criterion for salvation—namely, human achievement (3:3)—which lies outside God's way of salvation. To seek righteousness—which in this context does not refer to moral-ethical goodness, but conveys Paul's technical sense of "right relationship with God"—through observance of the law would be to "set aside the grace of God" (2:12).

Why is Paul so opposed to any intrusion of legal observance? One reason is worked out in the opening three chapters of Romans. While as a rabbi Paul seems clearly to have believed that complete obedience to the Mosaic law was possible (Phil 3:4-6), he was just as clearly convinced that such a path toward relationship with God led inevitably to self-righteousness, to pride in one's religious achievements, to boasting before others and God, and therefore to an implicit rejection of a stance of humility before the Creator. A second and perhaps more fundamental reason for rejecting the way of external, legalistic obedience was Paul's conviction that from the very beginning of redemptive history, the divinely established way toward saving relationship with God was by faith, not by works of the law (Gal 3:6-25; see also Rom 3—4).

On the basis of these convictions, Paul argues that if a system of law, even the Mosaic law, could impart life, then a right relationship with God "would certainly have come by the law" (3:21); but the only power the law has is to reveal our standing as sinners before a holy God and to show that we are finally dependent on his grace, receiving it in faith (3:18, 22-25).

That understanding of God's way of salvation, in contrast to the way of the Judaizers, elicits from Paul the charge that submission to circumcision [*as a means toward right standing before and with God*], means that Christ "is of no value" to them whatsoever (5:2). The bracketed phrase seeks to interpret Paul's meaning, in light of a parallel statement he makes in 2:21; namely, "if righteousness could be gained through the law, Christ died for nothing." The center of Paul's concern is of course that circumcision—which for Paul is "shorthand" for life lived in relation to the Mosaic law—understood and practiced *as a means to righteousness*, excludes the operation of God's grace. It is in fact the assertion that one can make it through personal achievement; as such it negates the necessity of the atonement.

For those who choose that way "Christ will be of no value," for the attempt "to be justified by law" leads to alienation from Christ and departure from grace. If we live "by the law," Christ and his atoning work have no value for us. But if we are "in Christ Jesus, neither circumcision nor uncircumcision has any value. The only thing that counts is faith expressing itself through love" (5:6).

• CHAPTER 34 •

The Israel of God

*Peace and mercy to all
who follow this rule,
even to the Israel of God.*
GALATIANS 6:16

Galatians 6:16 is part of Paul's benediction with which he closes the letter. Who is included among "the Israel of God"? What is "this rule"? The answer to the last question emerges quite naturally from the context. Based on differing understandings of both the structure of the sentence and Paul's terminology, opinions vary widely concerning the answer to the first.

Let us begin with the context. Paul has argued throughout this letter that God's way of salvation consists of his grace, offered in the atoning death of Jesus Christ through which persons are freed from the bondage of sin and legalistic religion. This redemptive work of God in Christ is appropriated in the response and life of faith. That thesis is worked out over against what can be called a judaizing faction among the Galatian Christians who believed and taught that right standing before God (that is, justification) is achieved, for Jews and Gentiles alike, only through adherence to the ritual of circumcision (and other parts of the ceremonial-ritual law).

This discussion is brought to a conclusion in the verses immediately preceding our saying (6:12-15). Those who insist on circumcision (which for Paul is here shorthand for religion under the law) are really seeking to establish an external measuring stick for human achievement before God on the basis of which one can boast (vv. 12-13). But, counters Paul, the only ground for "boasting" is outside us, namely, the cross of Christ (v. 14).

In such a case, boasting really becomes the praise of God for his unspeakable gift! That leads Paul to the sum of the matter: "Neither circumcision nor uncircumcision means anything; what counts is a new creation" (v. 15). That is, in the new creation inaugurated in Christ "there is neither Jew nor Greek" (Gal 3:28; see also 2 Cor 5:17). Neither the practice of external ritual or ceremony, nor its absence, is a basis for redemptive relationship with God. The only basis is the new creature, established by grace and through faith. That is the "rule" (or principle) to which Paul refers in our saying.

An understanding of the structure of the sentence, as well as the unique term "the Israel of God," is our second order of business. Notice first that the sentence punctuations in our English version, as well as in the Greek texts behind them, are the work of interpretation. Thus there are often a number of ways in which the text can be punctuated. And how one punctuates can determine the meaning or nuances of a text. In verse 16 there are basically two options, and slight variations within each of these.

1. The text used in this book (NIV), as well as most other

modern English versions, places the essential comma between two sentence parts: one contains the words "peace" and "mercy," the other contains the term "the Israel of God." This reading, based on the punctuation of the commonly accepted Greek text,[1] can be understood in at least two ways: (a) The benediction "peace and mercy" is pronounced on *one group.* "All who follow this rule," in part one of the sentence, are identified as "the Israel of God" in the second part of the sentence. Such a meaning is implied in our NIV reading of "even to the Israel of God," and the RSV's "unto the Israel of God." (b) The benediction is pronounced on *two groups,* those "who follow this rule" and the Israel of God. However, the term "Israel of God" is seen as a comprehensive term, *including* those in Galatia "who follow this rule." Among modern versions, TEV ("may peace and mercy be with them—with them and with all of God's people") and NEB ("and upon the whole Israel of God") support this understanding of the text.

2. Some commentators punctuate the Greek text differently.[2] It is grammatically possible to place the decisive comma so that the terms "peace" and "mercy" are separated as belonging to two distinct parts of the sentence. In that case it would read: "Peace to all who follow this rule, as well as [or, 'and'] mercy upon the Israel of God." On this reading, the benediction is divided and addresses two very distinct groups. "Peace" is pronounced upon believers in Christ ("those who follow this rule"); "mercy" is pronounced upon Israelites who are not yet, but may become, participants in the redeemed community of God's people.

The first option assumes that the term "Israel of God" is used by Paul for all those who are "in Christ," whether they are Jews or Gentiles. Since Paul uses the term only here, and it is found nowhere else in the entire New Testament, the use of it as synonymous with "Christian" must be derived from the broader Pauline context.

As in Galatians, so in Romans Paul argues that righteousness (right standing before God) comes by faith, not by works of the law. In Romans 4 he shows that way to have been God's way from the start. Proof is given in the example of Abraham, who believed God and thus came into right relationship with him before the external sign of circumcision was given (4:9-11). From this Paul draws the conclusion that Abraham "is the father of all who believe," both the uncircumcised (that is, Gentile believers— 4:11) and the circumcised (that is, Jewish believers—4:12). Since Abraham (the father of historical Israel) is also the father of all who believe, the designation of this company as the "Israel of God" would surely be appropriate (see also Rom 9:6-8).

Further support for such a correlation comes from Philippians, where Paul pointedly calls all those who put their faith in Christ Jesus "the circumcision" in contrast to those "who put [their] confidence in the flesh" (Phil 3:3), that is, who depend on their circumcision (Phil 3:4-6). In Galatians, too, "those who believe" are called "children of Abraham" (3:7), including Gentiles who respond in faith (3:8). This strand in Paul's thought is brought to a focal point in 3:26-29. Addressing the company of believers, consisting of both Jewish and Gentile believers, Paul says to them, "You are all sons of God through faith in Jesus Christ" (3:26). This designation is grounded in the Old Testament, where Israelites are called "sons of the living God" (Hos 1:10) or, collectively, "Son [of God]" (Hos 11:1). Here emerges the equation: Israel = son/sons of God = believers in Christ. Paul concludes the thought by affirming that those in Christ, both Jew and Gentile, are Abraham's offspring (3:27-29).

It would be difficult to deny that out of Paul's thought-development, briefly sketched above, the designation of the Christian fellowship as "Israel of God" could not have emerged. Thus there is a high degree of probability in this line of interpretation. Yet the second option outlined—which assigns to the term "Israel of

God" a more limited scope—has merit and should be given serious consideration.

In addition to seeing Abraham as "the father of all who believe" (Rom 4:11), Paul distinguished *two groups* within historic Israel. In Romans 2:28-29, he argues that there are two kinds of Jews: those who meet only the external requirements (circumcision and physical descent) and those who, in addition, are authentic Jews, inwardly, whose circumcision is not only external but also of the heart, worked "by the Spirit." To this idea of a "true" Israel within the historical, physical Israel may be assigned Paul's concept of the "remnant," which he explores in Romans 11. By God's grace, there are those within Israel who, like Paul, will yet respond in faith to God's work in Christ (11:1, 5). Is it possible, in light of this distinction between the whole people and the remnant, that Paul coined the term "Israel of God" to distinguish the remnant from simply "Israel"? If so, our text would receive a unique meaning. Paul's benediction of "peace" would be addressing "those who follow the rule," that is those who already belong to Christ. The benediction of "mercy" would be addressed to the faithful remnant within Israel, all those who had not yet grasped God's revelation in Jesus the Christ, but who by God's mercy would yet come to faith.

A final support for such an interpretation comes from the fact that the normal Pauline sequence in benediction and greetings is "grace and peace" (or "mercy and peace"), while here in 6:16 it is "peace and mercy." Since, according to Paul, God's mercy is that which leads to the condition of peace (with God, self and others), logical consistency would assign "peace" to those who are already in Christ, and "mercy" to those who are "not yet." That is plausible, with the reservation that greetings and benedictions are not always or necessarily logical formulations.

Whichever interpretation is accepted, one fact is clear; namely, Paul's overall view saw the church, the fellowship of God's people, as a new covenant community in which Jew and Greek, Israelite and Gentile, become one new people. And this people is the fulfillment of God's promise to Abraham at the beginning of redemptive history: "All the peoples on earth will be blessed through you" (Gen 12:3; Gal 3:29).

Notes

[1]The standard New Testament Greek text editions are those by Eberhard Nestlé and the United Bible Societies text (edited by Aland, Black, Metzger, Wikgren). It must be remembered that the punctuation is a result of the editors' decisions.

[2]For example, E. Burton, *The Epistle to the Galatians*, International Critical Commentary (New York: Scribner's Sons, 1970), pp. 357-58; also Duncan, *The Epistle of Paul to the Galatians* (London: Hodder and Stoughton, 1934), p. 192.

• C H A P T E R 3 5 •

Ascending
and
Descending

What does "he ascended" mean except that
he also descended to the lower earthly regions?
He who descended is the very one
who ascended higher than all the heavens,
in order to fill the whole universe.
EPHESIANS 4:9-10

T he section of the epistle in which Ephesians 4:9-10 is located makes
clear that the subject of the action referred to is Christ. But what
does the language of "ascending" and "descending" refer to?
What are the "lower earthly regions"? Are there various "heavens"? With what does he "fill the whole universe"?

These questions literally tumble out of the text at us. That is
particularly remarkable because the thrust of Paul's thought in
the total context of our passage is crystal clear. The obscurity of
our hard saying is at least partially due to the fact that the question in 4:10 ("What does 'he ascended' mean?") is in reference to
an Old Testament text cited in 4:8. Hoping to get a clue to Paul's

purpose in citing the text of Psalm 68:18, we read the text in its own setting. That, rather than helping, confuses even more when we realize that Paul cites the text with a significant alteration, apparently to make it fit his own purpose.

In the attempt to increase our understanding of the hard saying and gain greater clarity, we shall first look at the larger and immediate context, then explore Paul's use of the text from Psalm 68:18 (in 4:8), and lastly seek to understand Paul's "interpretation" of that text in applying it to Christ (in 4:9-10).

The central theological theme in the first four chapters of Ephesians is that the church of Jesus Christ is a creation of God in which a divided, fragmented humanity can be reconciled into one unified organism (1:22-23). The dividing wall between Jew and Gentile has been broken down (2:14-16). Those who were once "far off" (that is, Gentiles) have become part of the "household of God" which is being shaped into a "holy temple" in which God is present by his Spirit (2:17-22).

It is the unity and life and ministry of this "temple," this body of Christ which is the subject matter of chapter 4. After expressing the unity of the church in eloquent terms, grounding that unity in the fact that there is one Spirit, one Lord, one God and Father of all (4:1-6), Paul now moves on to acknowledge the body's diversity. Christ has given grace to the members of this body (4:7) for one purpose: that there would be apostles, prophets, evangelists, pastors and teachers (4:11) who would prepare all of God's people for service, so that the whole body would grow toward maturity, expressing in this world "the fullness of Christ" (4:12-13). It is the gifting of the church for its task which is the context for understanding Paul's reference to Psalm 68:18 and its application to Christ.

Paul moves from consideration of the unity of the church toward its diversity by stating that "to each one of us grace has been *given* as Christ has apportioned it" (or, more literally, "ac-

cording to the measure of Christ's *gift*"—4:7, emphasis mine).
Paul knew that the ascended, exalted Christ had poured out the
gift of the Spirit at Pentecost (Acts 2:32-38) and that by this
Spirit the church had been endowed with a variety of gifts (1 Cor
12:4-11).

As often in Paul's writings, a word or phrase or concept he is
presently using recalls for him a word from Scripture, which he
now proceeds to quote: "When he ascended on high, he led cap-
tives in his train and gave gifts to men." It is apparent that the
point of contact between what he has just written and the text
from Psalm 68:18 is that this text speaks of an exalted, victorious
one who gave gifts to his people. However, when we read the
Psalm verse in the Old Testament, we note that the victorious
one *"received gifts from men."* What is at first either disturbing or
puzzling is the impression that Paul alters the Old Testament
text to suit his purpose. A brief explanation should remove this
difficulty.

The Psalm quoted celebrates the victory of God over Israel's
enemies, and pictures that victory in terms of a triumphal procession to the sanctuary on Mount Zion, where the vanquished
bring their gifts of tribute to the victorious king, who receives
their gifts (68:17-18). This depiction of the triumph of God may
have struck Paul as expressing well the triumph of the messianic
king in cross, resurrection and exaltation. But since he thought
about the gifting of the church by the exalted Christ, and the
Psalm speaks of the exalted One receiving gifts from men, does
Paul simply alter the text? One answer has been that Paul may
neither have intended to quote exactly nor to interpet, "but in
familiar Jewish fashion adapts the passage to his own use, know-
ing that his readers . . . would recognize the alteration and see
the purpose of it."[1] That is possible. But there is another, and
likely better, explanation.

In Paul's time most Jews no longer understood Hebrew, Aramaic being their everyday language. In the synagogue, when the Hebrew text was read, a translator would freely render the text in a paraphrased form, often clarifying difficulties and making contemporary applications. These "interpretative translations" were handed down in oral form and later written down in what were called Targums. Now the Aramaic Targum text of Psalm 68:18 has precisely the change from "receiving gifts" to "giving gifts" which we find in Paul's quotation. It is quite possible that Paul simply makes use of the rabbinic interpretation of the Psalm passage. That interpretation may have arisen from the recognition that though the Psalm celebrates God's victory in analogy to the victory procession of earthly monarchs who receive gifts of homage and tribute from their conquered subjects, the exalted God of Israel is the one who bestows salvation on his people.

Having quoted the Psalm text, in keeping with its Targumic restatement, Paul now continues in typical rabbinic fashion to explore an aspect of the Psalm text in relation to the action of Christ, the messianic king who came and triumphed over death and was exalted to Lordship (Eph 1:20-21; see also Phil 2:5-11). Thus the words "he ascended" (from the Psalm), when applied to Christ, presuppose (or imply) "that he also descended to the lower, earthly regions" (4:9). What "descent" is in view here? And what are "the lower, earthly regions" (or, as in the NIV notes, "the depths of the earth")?

One view holds that Paul has in mind the Incarnation, the descent of the Son of Man from heaven to earth (see Jn 3:13). Within this view, there are two ways in which "the lower, earthly regions" can be understood: (1) It could be seen as a reference to the lowest parts of the earth, namely, the underworld—the world of the dead, Hades. That could refer simply to the fact that the descent of Christ climaxed in death and burial. Or it could be a reference to the idea found in the New Testament only in 1 Peter 3:18-20 that before his resurrection, Christ entered the world of the dead and preached to the departed spirits. (2) The phrase "lower, earthly regions" could be taken to mean "the lower, that is, earthly regions," in contrast to the height of heaven to which the Christ ascended (4:10).

An alternate view holds that the "ascent" precedes the "descent." In light of everything said previously in this epistle, Paul had no need to prove the Incarnation; that could be presupposed. Since the immediate context (vv. 7, 11) speaks about the giving of gifts to the church by the ascended, triumphant Lord, what Paul needed to show was that a descent was necessary in order for the exalted one to give these gifts. That descent is identified with the coming of Christ in the Spirit.

Paul's concept of the indwelling Christ (3:17) and John's teaching about the coming of Christ to the believers in the Spirit, subsequent to Jesus' "exaltation" (Jn 14:23-24), would support the possibility of such an understanding of the text.

However, since Paul nowhere speaks of the gift of the Spirit or the indwelling presence of Christ as a result of a "descent," it seems more probable that the well-established Pauline concept of Christ's humiliation and exaltation (Phil 2:5-11), in that order, stands behind the sequence in 4:9-10. This would admirably fit the context of the giving of Christ's gifts to the church. The one who emptied himself of divine glory and humbled himself even to death has been highly exalted "in order to fill the whole universe. It was he who gave . . ."

With what does he, literally, "fill the whole"? The TEV interprets the text to mean "fill the whole universe with his presence." RSV simply translates, "fill all things." Some have understood this "filling" in direct connection with the giving of the gifts, that is, he fills everything (or all) with his gifts.

Perhaps it is better to take the other common sense of the Greek word *plēroō* ("fill"), which is to "fulfill" or "bring to completion." That meaning would correspond well with a similar statement made earlier in the letter (1:23), where Paul speaks of the completion of the work of Christ. In that case, Paul speaks of Christ's descent (Incarnation) and ascent (Ascension, Exaltation) as having one purpose: to bring the mysterious purposes of God for humanity (Eph 1:8-10) to their completeness, to "fulfill" them. And the giving of gifts to the church is part of that "bringing all things to completion," since it is to lead to the church's perfection as expressing "the fullness of Christ" in the world.

Note

[1]T. K. Abbott, *Epistles to the Ephesians and Colossians*, International Critical Commentary (New York: Charles Scribner's Sons, 1897), p. 112.

CHAPTER 36

Wives, Submit

*Wives, submit to your husbands
as to the Lord.*
EPHESIANS 5:22

The difficulty of Ephesians 5:22 is not in understanding the rather straightforward language, but rather its meaning. Does it mean what it *seems* to convey, without regard to a serious consideration of the connections with the surrounding text, as well as the model for human relationships provided by the Lord's life? Since the patriarchal norms of the Greco-Roman world, built into the rules and regulations for everyday life and relationships, clearly demanded a wife's submission under the authority of the husband, is Paul simply advocating the continuance of conventional norms? If so, why would that be necessary? Does not the qualifying phrase, "as unto the Lord," introduce a radically new dimension into the nature and form of submission (or subordination)?

Of utmost importance for a proper grasp of Paul's intention are (1) the part this saying plays in the larger argument and (2) the specific meaning of terms and phrases in this saying and the surrounding text.

The larger context of this saying deals with Paul's concern that the believers, as a community and as individuals, would be strengthened by the Spirit of Christ (3:16-17) so that they would grow toward maturity (4:11-16). Such maturity comes as they are "kind and compassionate to one another" (4:32), living a life of love in imitation of God, as modeled in Christ's self-giving, sacrificial servant ministry (5:1-2).

How does this "imitation of Christ" work itself out concretely in the fellowship and common human relationships? That is the subject matter of Ephesians 5—6, and our text (5:22) is part of that.

A general discussion of Christian behavior under the admonition "Have nothing to do with the fruitless deeds of darkness" (5:3-16) is followed by more specific instructions regarding relationships in the fellowship and other social contexts, like the family. This section is introduced by the admonition "understand what the will of the Lord is. . . . Be filled with the Spirit" (5:17-18). Then, by means of four closely related participial phrases (5:19-21), he shows how the Spirit-filled and guided life, in tune with God's will, expresses itself: (1) "speaking with each other . . ." (2) "singing and making music . . ." (3) "giving thanks . . ." and (4) "submitting yourselves to one another . . ."[1] It is this last participial phrase which is critical for our understanding of 5:22.

Paul has clearly shown throughout the epistle that Christians are a new social order created to express the fullness of Christ in the midst of the old, fallen order. What he is saying in 5:21

is that the Spirit empowers Christians to exist in relationship with each other in a radical, culturally transforming way, namely, through mutual self-submission. The ground for this radically new approach to human relationships is "out of reverence for Christ." The reason for that reverence (or, perhaps better, awe) is the radical nature of Christ's earthly life, the total, free submission of himself as God's suffering servant, climaxed in his self-giving on the cross (5:2, 25). It is reverence and awe toward that self-giving love which is to motivate our mutual self-submission to each other.

This understanding of 5:21 ("Submit to one another") sheds critical light on 5:22 ("Wives, submit . . ."). Both the English translations and commentators often fail us at this point, either printing the participial clause of 5:21 as an isolated paragraph, separating it from both the preceding clauses and what follows (for example, NIV, NEB) or assigning 5:21 either to the preceding paragraphs (NASB) or to head a new paragraph (RSV, TEV). None of these do justice to the structure of the whole passage and to the grammar.

The participle of 5:21 ("submitting to one another") is the last of a series of four, as shown above, and clearly belongs to what precedes it. Verse 21 also supplies the verb "to submit" for our hard saying, without which 5:22 would be grammatically incomplete and without meaning. The verse in Greek reads literally: "Wives, to your husbands as to the Lord." The verb "to submit" is absent and can only be read into the sentence because of the intimate connection between the two verses. Verse 21 is therefore a transitional phrase, both belonging to what precedes and setting the agenda for what follows. Thus the kind of radical self-submission to one another (5:21) which evidences the fullness of the Spirit (5:18) is now explored in terms of its implications for husbands and wives (5:22-33). That is, what does this self-submission, modeled in Jesus, look like in marriage?

The submission of the wife to the husband is to be "as to the Lord." It is no longer to be the kind expected as a matter of course by cultural norms and forced upon women—who were seen as inferior to males in both Jewish and Gentile cultures. No, her submission is to be freely chosen, being there for her partner "as to the Lord," that is, as a disciple of the Lord, as one who followed in his servant footsteps, motivated by self-giving love. This kind of submission is not a reinforcement of the traditional norms; it is rather a fundamental challenge to them.

From much of Paul's correspondence we can see that the new freedom from restrictive and often enslaving cultural norms brought by the gospel led at times to rejection of the very relationships in which these norms had been operative, such as marriage itself. It is that danger which Paul may be addressing in 5:23. Appealing to the creation account in Genesis 2, where the woman is created out of the being of the male (2:21-23), Paul says, "For the husband [man] is the head of the wife [woman]."

We discussed Paul's use of the word *head* in chapter 22. We discovered there that in common Greek the idea of "authority over" was not normally conveyed by the word *head (kephalē)*. Besides its literal, physical meaning ("head of man or beast"), it had numerous metaphorical meanings, including that of "source." It is this meaning of *kephalē* which seems most suited to the texts (1 Cor 11:3 and Eph 5:23) in which the relationship of husband and wife (or man and woman) is addressed.[2]

In both texts, appeal is made to Genesis 2, where the woman is created from the male. Thus Paul, in arguing against those who would reject the marriage relationship because of a new freedom in Christ (see Gal 3:28), reminds them that, according to God's design, the man is the source of the woman's being; they were created for each other and belong together, as Ephesians 5:31, citing Genesis 2:24, underlines. Similarly (and here begins the analogy between husband/wife—Christ/church), Christ is the *kephalē* ("source") of the church's life (5:23). His relation to the church is not expressed in "authority" language," but in "source" language. Christ is the church's savior because he laid down his life for her.

A final argument for the validity of a radically new self-submission of wife to husband is now given: "As the church submits to Christ, so also wives to their husbands in everything" (5:24). What is the nature of the church's submission to Christ? It is freely assumed in humble response to his self-giving, sacrificial servanthood and his continuing empowering and nurturing presence. The church's submission to Christ has nothing to do with external control or coercion. For the life and ministry of Jesus demonstrates uncompromisingly his rejection of "power over others" as valid in the new creation which he is inaugurating (Lk 22:24-27).[3] Christ stands in relation to the church, his bride, not as one who uses his power to control and demand, but rather to invite and serve.

Having radically challenged the nature of the culturally expected and demanded submission of the wife to the husband, Paul now goes on (5:25-32) to show what self-submission by the husband to the wife looks like in practice. The husband's self-submission (5:21) is to express itself in the kind of radical self-giving love which Christ demonstrated when "he gave himself up for" the life of the church (5:25). Husbands were of course expected to have erotic regard for their wives. But within a culture in which women were often not more than doormats on which male supremacy could wipe its feet, and in a religious setting where Jewish males thanked God daily that he had not made them a Gentile, a slave or a woman—in such a context erotic regard for the wife more often than not became a means of self-gratification and control over the wife. That position of superiority is daringly challenged by Paul's call upon husbands to love (*agapaō*) their wives, that is to be there for them and with them in self-giving, nurturing, serving love. For that is the way Christ loved the church, and husbands, like their wives, are to be imitators of Christ (Eph 5:2).

Notes

[1]For an excellent discussion of the meaning of these four participial phrases, see Markus Barth, *Epistle to the Ephesians*, The Anchor Bible, 2 vols. (New York: Doubleday, 1974), 2:583-85.

[2]In Ephesians 4:15-16 the Greek word *kephalē* ("head") is also used with the metaphorical meaning of "source." Christ is the "head" (that is, source) from whom the whole body grows and upbuilds itself in love. In the physiology of the period, the physical head was understood to give life to the rest of the body.

[3]See also Mark 8:31-38; 9:30-37; 10:32-45; John 13:12-17; Philippians 2:5-11.

• C H A P T E R 3 7 •

Work Out Your Salvation

*Continue to work out your salvation
with fear and trembling,
for it is God who works in you
to will and to act according
to his good purpose.*
PHILIPPIANS 2:12-13

Philippians 2:12-13 *is difficult only when we do not hear it within* the context of everything else Paul says about God's work of redemption and our involvement in that work. Certainly since the Reformation, when the essence of Paul's gospel was captured in the joyful proclamation *sola gratia, sola fide* ("by grace alone, by faith alone"), anything which even hints at "works righteousness" or "salvation by works" is suspect. And that is the concern which often emerges when believers read Philippians 2:12-13.

This concern can be put to rest, for a careful look at Paul's teaching on all aspects of God's redemptive work in Christ reveals that salvation is not based on the accumulated merits of our piety and good deeds. No, salvation is God's business from beginning to end. It is inaugurated, maintained and completed by him. Yet we human beings, the objects of that divine activity, are not robots manipulated by the divine button-pusher. We are creatures created in God's image (Gen 1:26-27), called to respond in faith and love to the Creator and to give ourselves in active participation to God's purposes. It is this dual perspective of divine action and human response and participation which is in view in this text.

The center of Paul's proclamation, repeated in numerous ways throughout his writings, is most concisely and eloquently stated in Ephesians 2:8-9: "For it is by grace you have been saved, through faith—and this not from yourselves, it is the gift of God—not by works, so that no one can boast." The meaning is without ambiguity; there are no conditions imposed (such as "if . . . then"). God reaching toward us in unconditional love (Rom 5:8) is all grace. We neither deserve it nor earn it, and therefore we cannot take credit for it ("so that no one can boast"). The verb "you have been saved" is in the perfect tense and the passive voice, which means that the action comes from outside ourselves and that it is something which is both an accomplished act and a reality which continues in its effectiveness through the present and into the future.

Now this strong affirmation is immediately followed in 2:10 by the words: "For we are God's workmanship, created in Christ Jesus to do good works . . ." Here, as throughout his letters, Paul is very clear about the fact that restored relationship with God is the condition within which our lives are being transformed in such a way that God's purposes for our lives are brought about. A few examples will make this abundantly clear.

In Romans 6 believers are defined as those who have been baptized into Christ, buried with him and raised with him so that we "might walk in newness of life" (6:3-4). Here the transaction of being saved is pictured as accomplished fact; the "walking in newness of life," as a possibility yet to be realized. Then Paul goes on to say that our sinful self has been "crucified with" Christ, that we are no longer "enslaved to sin" (6:5-11).

The affirmation of this accomplished fact is then immediately followed by the imperative: "Do not let sin therefore reign. . . . Do not offer [yourselves] to sin as instruments of wickedness . . . but rather to God . . . as instruments of righteousness" (6:12-13).

In Galatians, where salvation by faith in Christ is particularly stressed (for example, in 2:16: "a man is not justified by observing the law but by faith in Jesus Christ"), Paul can also stress that "in Christ," that is, in our relationship to God in Christ, what really matters is "faith expressing itself through love" (5:6). Therefore, "serve one another in love" (5:13).

The seeming tension between affirmations of accomplished salvation and a life in which a new reality is expressed and put to work is partially due to the fact that Paul's use of particular words or expressions is somewhat flexible. In our text, salvation is a reality still in process and yet to be accomplished. In Romans 1:16 and Ephesians 1:13 the term *salvation* is used in a general, comprehensive sense, and as a synonym for *gospel* (that is, the good news of, and power for, salvation). In 2 Corinthians 7:10, repentance is said to lead to salvation. There are other texts in which salvation is depicted as the final stage or event in the redemptive activity of God. The Thessalonians are told that they were chosen "to be saved through the sanctifying work of the Spirit" (2 Thess 2:13) and that one piece of the Christian's armor against the darkness was "the hope of salvation" (1 Thess 5:8). The clearest example of the futuristic use of the term is in Romans 13:11, where we hear that "salvation is nearer now than when we first believed."

When we take all these aspects together, we see that Paul

thought of salvation as the totality of God's redemptive work; yet he freely used the term also to denote various parts of the whole. The best illustration of Paul's understanding of salvation in its totality, described in terms of its various stages, is found in Romans 5. We "have been justified through faith" (5:1). To be justified—Paul's most usual term for what happens to us when we respond in faith to God's love in Christ—is to be brought into right relationship with God, a condition he describes as "peace with God" (5:1). The culmination of that which has thus begun is sharing "the glory of God" (5:2). Between these two poles, Christian life is characterized by joy in the midst of adversity, hope in the midst of suffering (5:3-5), because, having been justified by Christ's sacrificial death (5:9), the continuing work of the resurrected Lord in the life of the believer will lead to final salvation (5:10).

The larger context for our saying, as worked out above, consists of three elements: (1) the duality of "already" and "not yet"; (2) the *actuality of restored relation with God* and the necessity of living in newness of life; (3) the understanding of salvation as the comprehensive work of God in which we participate through faith, hope and love. Within this context, Philippians 2:12-13 is best understood.

He calls his readers to unity in their common life, to be achieved through humble other-directedness (Phil 2:1-4), motivated by the example of Christ's humiliation and utter self-giving (2:5-11). It is this work of Christ which for Paul is the basis ("therefore") of the imperative "now work out your salvation with fear and trembling" (2:12). The salvation which comes to us through Christ's "obedience to death" (2:8) is to be "incarnated," implemented and worked out, within the context of our relationships with each other. The motivation for this "outworking" is "fear and trembling," not in the sense of "being afraid of," but rather in the sense of "awe," namely, the "awe" which comes when we contemplate God's work of "amazing grace" in Christ.

But this "outworking of salvation" in our human contexts—in Philippi toward unity within the congregation—is not "human achievement" on the basis of which we can "boast." No, for this outworking of salvation is empowered by the continuing operation of God's grace, for God is at work "in you" (or "among you").

Salvation is not something we possess. It is rather a relationship in which we stand. And within that relationship, we become partakers of God's Spirit. Thus Christian action is never "our work"; it is always the outgrowth of a dynamic relationship, whose author and completer is God.

CHAPTER 38

Faultless before the Law

If anyone else thinks he has reasons
to put confidence in the flesh,
I have more. . . . As for legalistic
righteousness, faultless.
PHILIPPIANS 3:4-6

What strikes us immediately about Philippians 3:4-6 is the sense of superiority which it seems to convey, as well as Paul's lofty claim about his moral and religious perfection. The tone of this statement seems somehow unbecoming the "apostle to the Gentiles." Did he not say, earlier in this same letter, that a Christlike spirit leads one to consider others better than oneself (2:3)? And isn't this the same apostle who invested much of his energy showing that boasting on the basis of human achievement—even in religious practice and moral righteousness—was a hindrance to relationship with God? As to the claim to faultlessness regarding the Mosaic Law, did he not also spend a great deal of energy showing that perfection under the Law was impossible, that "all have sinned and fallen short of the glory of God" (Rom 3:23)?

The situation addressed in this text, as well as in two other letters where a similar tone emerges (2 Cor 10—12; Gal 1—3), shows that Paul is involved in a polemical situation where he carries on a debate with opponents whose teachings or response to Paul's apostolic authority threaten congregational life or the integrity of his gospel. What often characterizes polemical rhetoric is irony, or hyperbole, or both. One side of the argument is overstated in order to reveal the absurdity or error of the other side. Or the opponents and their position are pilloried in the worst possible light in order to drive home the main point of the argument.

These rhetorical, literary devices account for the tone of superiority conveyed in our text. Paul is either arguing against the Judaizers (see chapter 32 above)—those Jewish Christians who continued to demand that both Jewish and Gentile Christians adhere to the rite of circumcision and the ritual law—or against representatives of the synagogue—who opposed Paul's proclamation in Macedonia from the very beginning (see Acts 16:1—17:15).[1] He calls his opponents in Philippi "dogs," an epithet of derision commonly used by Jews against Gentiles, now turned against his own people. In a caustic word play in reference to the rite of circumcision (peritomē), he labels them "mutilators of the flesh" (katatomē, 3:2). That this is polemical rhetoric is clear in light of the fact that these are the same people for whom Paul has deep compassion and in exchange for whose salvation he is willing to be "cursed and cut off from Christ" (Rom 9:3).

Within this polemic Paul now, in a twist of irony, assumes their point of view and argues on their terms to show that even at its best, the way of achievement under the Law does not lead to authentic relationship with God. To insist on the accumulation of merit before God by adhering to the meticulous precepts of the ritual law of Judaism is "to put confidence in the flesh" (3:3). The term *flesh* here denotes human ability, the capacity apart from dependence on God to live life in such a way that God is pleased. If that is the standard by which one is ultimately measured, says Paul, then I have as much reason as anyone, perhaps more, to be confident (3:4).

The list of qualifying credentials which follows—"circumcised on the eighth day, of the people of Israel, of the tribe of Benjamin, a Hebrew of Hebrews; in regard to the law, a Pharisee; as for zeal, persecuting the church" (3:5-6)—emphasizes his natural credentials, the ritualistic accuracy of acts performed ("on the eighth day!" as required by Levitical Law) and his personal achievements. This latter is expressed first of all in the phrase "in regard to the law, a Pharisee."

Though we have come virtually to equate "Pharisee" with "hypocrite" (largely by generalizing Jesus' denunciation of those Pharisees who opposed his ministry as hypocrites—Mt 23:13), to be a member of the religious party of the Pharisees was a badge of honor. We know from Jewish sources that these religious leaders were extremely meticulous about the observance of the Mosaic Law and its interpretations which had been handed down for centuries.[2] It was the Pharisees who believed that if all Jews would keep the Law perfectly for just one day, the kingdom of God would come. Thus it was their lofty goal to lead Israel to perfect obedience. Many were deeply pious and earnest about the accomplishment of God's will as they understood it. For many others that same effort became a source of pride and self-righteousness (see Rom 10:2-3). I, says Paul, was one of these Pharisees.

In addition, his zeal for the Law as a Pharisee expressed itself in his persecution of those who claimed that the one who had been rejected by the Pharisees was the expected Messiah (3:6; see also Gal 1:13-14). For him this new faith threatened the inherited tradition, and he saw himself as the defender of that tradition.

The ultimate claim on which "confidence in the flesh" could be based is now made, namely, legalistic perfection. Paul the Pharisee, schooled by the rabbis in the traditions of the Law, was convinced that in all respects he had adhered to the letter of the Law; he had kept the myriad rules and regulations which had been established in order to keep the faithful from disobeying the Law of Moses. Paul echoes here the words of the young man who, in response to Jesus' question about the commandments, says in absolute confidence: "All these I have kept since I was a boy" (Lk 18:20-21).

Paul shared the conviction of his fellow rabbis that it was possible to keep the Law and that he had, in fact, mastered it.[3] Though this affirmation may at first sight appear to contradict other statements Paul makes (see Rom 2:17-24; 7:7-20), it is quite consistent with his belief that even if one were able to keep the entire Law, one would not be justified (that is, come into right relationship with God) on that basis (Gal 2:16-17; 3:21). Surely Paul's experience of being grasped by Christ on the Damascus road led to this assessment. In the ultimate act of zealousness for the Law—namely, the persecution of Jesus' followers—he found himself to be opposing the very purposes of God. He discovered that confidence in one's ability to prove oneself worthy in God's sight has the effect of separating one from God. Why? Because it implicitly rejects humble dependence on God. Only in faith— in dependence on God—can one be open, both to an understanding of God's purposes and to God's empowerment for participating in those purposes.

Notes

[1]For example, F. W. Beare, *A Commentary on the Epistle to the Philippians,* Harper's New Testament Commentaries (New York: Harper & Brothers, Publishers, 1959), pp. 103-5.

[2]For one of the best treatments of Judaism in the New Testament period and a comprehensive understanding of the religious sects and their beliefs, see G. F. Moore, *Judaism in the First Centuries of the Christian Era*, 2 vols. (Cambridge, Mass.: Harvard University Press, 1927).

[3]E. P. Sanders, *Paul and Palestinian Judaism* (Philadelphia: Fortress Press, 1977).

CHAPTER 39

The Firstborn over Creation

*He is the image
of the invisible God,
the firstborn over all creation.*
COLOSSIANS 1:15

Colossians 1:15, and the passage surrounding it (1:15-20), is among
the most important New Testament presentations of the nature
and person of Christ. From the time of Jesus' ministry through
the writing of the New Testament and into the centuries beyond
when Christian thinkers hammered out the basic creeds of the
faith, understanding the identity of Jesus Christ was a central
concern.

In answer to Jesus' question "Who do you say I am?" Peter
responds, "You are the Christ" (Mk 8:29). Jesus acknowledges
this confession as valid (see also Mt 16:16-17), but when it becomes clear that Peter understands Jesus' identity as Messiah in

primarily political, triumphalistic terms, he is rebuked by the Lord, for the true Messiah must endure suffering and death (Mk 8:30-38). And from Peter onward, as evidenced in the pages of the New Testament, the identity of Jesus was revealed with increasing clarity and proclaimed with increasing understanding and conviction.

Our passage is one among several of Paul's responses to the question he asked when first encountered by Christ on the Damascus road: "Who are you, Lord?" (Acts 9:5). These responses come to us in varied form and terminology, revealing various aspects of early Christian belief about this One through whose life, death and resurrection a new era had dawned. Neither for Jesus' original followers nor for those like Paul who became followers after Jesus' resurrection was an understanding of Jesus' full identity there from the beginning. They grew in faith and knowledge as they "searched the Scriptures" (our Old Testament), convinced that they bore witness to Jesus' identity (see Jn 5:39). It is thus no accident that the confessions about him are steeped in Old Testament images and terms.

The letter to the Christians in Colossae—written from prison in Rome toward the end of Paul's life—contains perhaps the most mature and complete response to the question about who Jesus was and is. The entire passage which begins with our text (1:15-20) contains more lofty affirmations about Christ than any other text in the New Testament. Our efforts toward greater clarity will concentrate on the two prominent definitions which are given, namely, "image" of God and "firstborn" over all creation.

In the New Testament, only Paul uses the word *image* (Greek, *eikōn*) to designate a reflection, an "imaging," of a personal reality in another person or persons. In clear dependence on Genesis 1:26-27, Paul speaks of man as the "image of God" (1 Cor 11:7) and of the Christian as one who is being renewed "in the image of its Creator" (Col 3:10). This basic biblical conviction that the human being, in some mysterious sense, reflects the reality of God, becomes for Paul the basis for another use of the "image" metaphor. Christians are intended "to be conformed to the image of his Son" (Rom 8:29). They shall "bear the image of the man from heaven" (1 Cor 15:49) and "are being changed into his [Christ's] image" (2 Cor 3:18).

Paul's belief that Christians are being transformed into Christ's image rests on two related convictions. The first is that the human creation, as "image of God," is distorted by sin. Human life does not, as intended, reflect God's steadfast love and faithfulness, the essence of God's relational nature. The second conviction is that in Christ the "image of God" is truly revealed and present: The "glory of God" is reflected "in the face of Christ" (2 Cor 4:6) because he is "the image of God" (2 Cor 4:4). That conviction is heightened in our text: The "invisible" nature of God has become "visible" in the Incarnation, for Christ is the image of God (Col 1:15). What Adam (as representative of all human beings) was created to be, but in the deepest sense failed to become because of sin—namely, the "image of God" (Gen 1:26-27)—Christ, the incarnate one, truly was and is.

For Paul, Adam and Christ are representative of two orders of humanity (see Rom 5:15-17; 1 Cor 15:45-46): Adam of the original creation, Christ of the new creation; Adam of the creation marred by sin, Christ of the new creation freed from sin's bondage. Therefore, what human beings "in Adam" were created to be but failed to be in their lives (that is, the image of God), human beings "in Christ" (who is the true image of God) are destined to become.

The second, and more difficult, concept of our Colossians text, is that of Christ as the "firstborn" of all creation. The potential problem of this term as applied to Christ is the question it seems to raise about Christ's eternal nature. If he was "firstborn," was there ever a time when he did not exist?

The term *firstborn* is found several times in the New Testament. Twice it is employed in the common sense, in reference to the first child born to a woman (Lk 2:7; Heb 11:28). From this "natural" sense is derived its metaphorical use, where "firstborn" is a designation of "first" among many others to follow. Jesus, as the resurrected one, is "the firstborn" from the dead, because Christians too will be raised from the dead (Col 1:18; Rev 1:5). He is also "the firstborn among many brothers" in God's new order, for Christians are destined to be conformed to the image of God's Son (Rom 8:29). As a designation of Christ, without reference to anything or anyone else, "firstborn" is used in Hebrews 1:6. Here, as in our text, it is almost used as a title for Christ. What meaning or meanings does this designation convey?

In Exodus 4:22 and Jeremiah 31:9, Israel is called God's "firstborn," and in Psalm 89:27, David the king is called God's "firstborn, the most exalted of the kings of the earth." In neither of these uses of the term is conveyed the sense "first in a series" or "the first who is born from." In reference to Israel, the designation signifies importance, uniqueness. God chose Israel as his peculiar people for a redemptive mission. He loves Israel with that special kind of love which parents experience when that first child is born (see Hos 11:1). In reference to David, the term *firstborn* is defined for us in the next line of the Psalm: he is "most exalted of the kings of the earth." *Firstborn* is here but a metaphor for "exalted one."

Since in rabbinic interpretation Psalm 89 was not only read in relation to King David, but also in reference to the coming Messiah, the Psalm's use of *firstborn* could be the basis for the term's application to Christ in the epistles to the Hebrews and the Colossians.

It is possible that a messianic reading of Psalm 89 carried the connotation of "exalted one" into Paul's use of "firstborn" in

Colossians 1:15. Such a meaning would certainly be in keeping with early Christian convictions regarding the exaltation of the resurrected Lord to a position of authority (Acts 2:33-36; Phil 2:9-11). The NIV rendering "firstborn *over* all creation," certainly supports this sense of exaltation, supremacy, sovereignty.

It is also possible, however, that the genitive construction of 1:15 is to be understood in its most common sense. In that case, we would read "firstborn *of* all creation" (so NASB and RSV). The emphasis would here be on priority in time and unique distinction from the created order. Such a significance for "firstborn" would be supported by the statements in 1:16 ("by him all things were created") and 1:17 ("He is before all things"). In light of these further affirmations about Christ, it is impossible to hold that Christ as "firstborn" is included in the comprehensive "all creation." The pre-eminence of Christ in relation to all created reality is affirmed unambiguously throughout this text. Only of him is it said that the fullness of God dwells in him and is expressed through him (1:19; 2:9).

Paul's exposition of Christ as "image of the invisible God" and "firstborn over [or 'of'] all creation" is directed against false teachers who, among other things, advocate the worship of angelic beings (Col 2:8-23). If, as some have maintained throughout church history, "firstborn" designates Christ as a created being and "image of God" affirms Christ's true humanity (in keeping with Gen 1:26-27), then Paul could hardly have criticized those in Colossae who advocated the worship of supernatural, angelic powers. But the very fact that he is involved in a polemic against such teaching confirms that his exposition of Christ's uniqueness and exalted status intends to discredit any claims about the worthiness of other objects of worship.

Christ is "image of God" in a way in which Adam (and all human beings) never was and could be, for in that "image" the completeness of God's being is expressed. Christ is "the firstborn," not in the sense of one who is born or created as first among others, but as one who is *prior* to all created orders and exalted above them. This text therefore affirms the eternity of Christ no less than the Gospel of John's teaching about Christ as the eternal word of God which was "with God in the beginning" (Jn 1:1-2).

CHAPTER 40

What Is Lacking in Christ's Afflictions

*Now I rejoice in what was suffered
for you, and I fill up in my flesh
what is still lacking in regard to Christ's
afflictions, for the sake of his body,
which is the church.*
COLOSSIANS 1:24

The phrases *"what is still lacking"* and *"Christ's afflictions"* from Colossians 1:24 confront us with several difficulties. On the surface they seem to imply that there is some sort of deficiency in Christ's sufferings, that the effectiveness of our Lord's suffering is somehow limited and that its redemptive purpose must be supplemented or completed by Paul's suffering. In addition to this central problem, there is the question of how Paul's suffering can be "for the sake of" the church, especially since the church at Colossae was not established by Paul nor had he visited it (1:3-8).

In light of everything else which Paul affirms about the redemptive significance of Christ's life, death and resurrection, it is virtually impossible to attribute to him the idea that this redemptive work is in some way incomplete. Even within the immediate context, Paul clearly articulates the finality of God's saving action in Christ. In the cross, Christ triumphed over all those powers of sin and bondage and death which separate us from God and his purposes (2:13-15). As a result of the proclamation of the gospel, Christians are those who have been rescued from the dominion of darkness and brought into the kingdom of God's Son (1:13), through whom redemption and forgiveness of sins has been bestowed (1:14). Though once alienated from God, they have been reconciled to God by Christ's death (1:22).

This sense of the finality, absolute completeness and all-sufficiency of Christ's vicarious suffering is confirmed both by other key texts from Paul's hand and by the terms which he normally uses when he speaks of Christ's atoning work. Among the many passages which could be cited is Romans 5:1, 10, where justification and reconciliation, as results of Christ's death, are described as accomplished facts (see also Gal 4:1-7; 1 Cor 1:21-30; Eph 1:7, 13-14). In addition to this larger evidence from his epistles, Paul's normal way of speaking about Christ's redemptive work is in terms of his death, his blood, his cross or a combination of these terms (see Rom 5:8-9; Col 1:20). The expression "Christ's afflictions" is nowhere else attested as a reference to his saving work.

What then can be the meaning of this enigmatic expression? In what sense are "Christ's afflictions" incomplete? How do Paul's sufferings "fill up" that incompleteness? Several interpretations have been proposed.[1] One holds that the word *afflictions* is a reference to Paul's sufferings and that the genitive "of Christ" is to be taken in an objective sense, that is, meaning "for the sake of Christ." The sentence would then read: "I rejoice in what was suffered for you, and I fill up in my flesh what is still

lacking in [my] afflictions for the sake of Christ." This idea that
Paul saw his own sufferings as being endured for the sake of
Christ is certainly present in his experience (see Acts 9:16; 2 Cor
4:10-11). The attractiveness of this interpretation is hindered by
the fact that the term "of the afflictions" goes most naturally
with "of Christ" in the grammatical construction, and thus
means "the afflictions of Christ." The proposed interpretation
also does not adequately explain how what is yet to be filled up
in Paul's afflictions is for the benefit of the church.

An alternative to the above way of dealing with the problem
is to understand the genitive, "of Christ," as a reference to the
nature of Christ's suffering. Paul's sufferings are "like those of
Christ." But how the model of Christ's sufferings, now experienced by Paul, is deficient and is to be "filled up," is not answered by this explanation.

A more satisfactory understanding of our passage has been
suggested by recent studies which seek to take seriously the
background of Paul's terminology in the Old Testament and in
the apocalyptic literature[2] of intertestamental Judaism. Within that
background, there are several related concepts which parallel
those in our passage: (1) Israel's experience of affliction throughout its history—particularly Egyptian slavery, Babylonian exile,
and subsequent oppression under the Syrians and Romans—is
understood as part and parcel of God's redemptive purposes.
Within this larger frame, the sufferings of God's righteous ones,
God's special servants (Ps 34:19; 37:39; 50:15), were often taken
as representative and vicarious (for example, Is 53). (2) In the
apocalyptic literature, beginning with Daniel 12:1, the time prior
to the culmination of God's redemptive work and the inaugura-
tion of the reign of God in the messianic age, was depicted as a
period of great affliction. These afflictions were known as "the
woes of the Messiah," not referring to sufferings to be endured
by the Messiah, but to afflictions out of which the messianic age

would be born. (3) Finally the apocalyptic seers announced that
this present age of suffering was limited, that the "age to come"
would soon dawn and that God had determined a definite measure for the afflictions that had to be experienced.[3]

These elements of Paul's Jewish background help us to understand our hard saying. Paul was certainly convinced that the final
days had dawned (1 Cor 7:29) and that the present time was one
of difficulty and crisis (1 Cor 7:26). Christians are those "upon
whom the end of the ages has come" (1 Cor 10:11) and who are
therefore participants with Christ (the Messiah) in his sufferings
as a prelude to sharing in the glory of his reign (Rom 8:17-18).
Within this larger view, the difficult concepts of our passage can
be understood.

The "afflictions of Christ" may be a reference to the "woes of
the Messiah"; namely, the sufferings experienced by God's people in the last days. Paul's own sufferings, experienced in his
missionary work (see 2 Cor 1:3-6), would then be seen as a part
of this suffering of Christ's followers. The phrase "fill up what
is still lacking" may be in direct correspondence to the apocalyptic
notion that a definite limit has been set by God to the sufferings
to be endured. Paul could be expressing the conviction that his
sufferings, alongside the sufferings of God's people generally
(see 2 Cor 1:6), contribute to the total measure of afflictions
determined by God. Thus his sufferings are "for the sake of the
church," since they hasten the day when the church's present
affliction will be replaced by glory.

Though understanding our text within the larger apocalyptic
view of "the afflictions of the Messiah" solves the various difficulties identified at the outset of this chapter, a more direct explanation may suggest itself from within Paul's own thought.

As shown above, there can be no question that Christ's sufferings, climaxed in the cross, are all-sufficient. Peace, reconciliation, right standing with God are its results. At the same time

Paul is also convinced that this gospel must be proclaimed, received in faith and implemented in everyday life in order for God's redemptive purposes to be achieved. Thus, within the immediate context of our passage, the good news of Christ's death which the Colossian Christians heard (1:22-23) is intended to bear fruit in their lives (1:6) and to lead to a life pleasing to the Lord (1:10) that is characterized by endurance and patience (1:11), continuing faith (1:23) and unity in love (2:2). The ultimate purpose of Christ's atoning death is to present holy and without blemish to God those who have received redemption (1:14, 22). Paul's work as a servant of the gospel of Christ is part of God's means to accomplish that purpose (1:23).

Elsewhere Paul affirms that the good news of Christ's saving death can only be heard and believed if it is proclaimed (Rom 10:14-17), and he knows himself to be a proclaimer of that good news (1 Cor 1:17-23), as well as one whose life is an imitation of Christ's self-giving love on behalf of others (Eph 5:1-2; 1 Cor 10:33—11:1). All of this does not mean that there is something lacking in Christ's redemptive work, but rather that Paul's and others' servant ministry, which includes suffering, is an integral part of bringing redemption to all. Such a sense for Colossians 1:24 is supported by a very similar text, 2 Cor 1:5-6.

In 2 Corinthians 1:5-6 Paul affirms that Christ's sufferings are extended in his own and that this suffering is "for the sake of" the Corinthian believers' salvation. Paul's suffering in the service of Christ and his gospel do not add anything to the perfection of Christ's atonement. They are, however, one of God's instruments to extend that atonement into the lives of others. Only in that sense can it be said that Paul's sufferings fill up what is lacking in regard to Christ's afflictions.

Notes

[1]Extensive discussions of various interpretations can be found in the

commentaries on this epistle. A good example is Peter T. O'Brian, *Colossians, Philemon*, Word Biblical Commentary 44 (Waco, Tex.: Word, 1987), pp. 77-78.

[2]From approximately 200 B.C. to A.D. 100 there appeared an extensive religious literature which, like the canonical Daniel, sought to give hope to an oppressed, persecuted and suffering people. Various concepts of this literature, which revealed *(apokalyptō)* the purposes of God, were very much a part of Jesus' understanding of his person and mission, as well as Paul's interpretation of Christ's work and its significance for Christian living. O'Brian, *Colossians, Philemon*, pp. 78-81, gives a detailed analysis of this literature's concepts relating to our passage.

[3]As examples of this element in Jewish apocalyptic writings, see 1 Enoch 47:1-4, Baruch 30:2 and 4 Ezra 4:36-37 in R. H. Charles, ed., *The Apocrypha and Pseudepigrapha of the Old Testament*, vol. 2.

• C H A P T E R   4 1 •

Anti-
Semitic?

*The Jews . . . displease God
and are hostile to all men.*
1 THESSALONIANS 2:14-15

Throughout the history of Jewish-Christian relations, 1 Thessalonians 2:14-15 and several other passages in the New Testament, like John 8:44, have been used all too frequently as a justification for inappropriate attitudes and actions toward Jewish people. Those actions and attitudes are called anti-Semitic. A dictionary definition of anti-Semitism includes such terms as "prejudice against Jews; dislike or fear of Jews; discrimination against or persecution of Jews."[1] Such anti-Semitism on the part of Christians has led to the charge that the New Testament, or at least certain writers of New Testament Gospels or Epistles, were anti-Semitic. Can the use of 1 Thessalonians 2:14-15 (and others) for anti-

Semitic attitudes and actions, or the charge that these texts are in themselves anti-Semitic, be justified?

First, it should be noted that these so-called anti-Semitic statements come from persons who were themselves Semites. They were not uttered by Gentiles hostile to Jews or to Jewish customs or beliefs. Their Jewishness and their commitment to the sacred writings which give to Judaism its uniqueness and identity are affirmed. Thus Jesus points to the Jewish Scriptures as bearing witness to him (Jn 5:39); and throughout John's Gospel, Jesus' identity as Messiah, as the royal Son of God, is prominent. In the same vein, Paul repeatedly underlines his Jewishness, his belonging to the people who trace their ancestry to Abraham (Rom 11:1; Gal 1:13-14; Phil 3:4-6).

Not only do we have an affirmation of Jewish identity, but that identity is expressed in powerfully positive ways. Throughout the Gospel record, Jesus' love and compassion for his own people is amply demonstrated. A particularly tender expression of it is found in Jesus' lament over Jerusalem: "How often I have longed to gather your children together, as a hen gathers her chicks under her wings" (Lk 13:34). Paul parallels this deep yearning for the wholeness and salvation of his own people when he expresses his deep sorrow over Israel's rejection of Christ and his willingness even to be cursed for their sake (Rom 9:2-3). In addition, Paul sees the rejection of the Messiah by his own people as but a temporary reality. He knows that God has not rejected his own people (Rom 11:7) and envisions a time when they will be grafted back into God's olive tree (Rom 11:17-24).

In the context of this larger picture in the New Testament, we are now ready to look at our specific text. Paul's rather strong words are elicited by a situation in Thessalonica in which Christians (probably gentile Christians) are suffering at the hands of their own countrymen (2:14). The new faith, based on the gospel of Jesus Christ, is being opposed in Thessalonica, just as it was being opposed in the Judean churches, by their countrymen, namely, their fellow Jews (2:14). To this point in the text, Paul has not singled out any national group. The gospel is opposed by both Greeks and Jews, and those committed to it are liable to persecution. It is the following verse (2:15) which singles out "the Jews" for special denunciation: "They displease God and are hostile to all men."

This statement has the same anti-Semitic flavor as the rather slanderous remarks made against Jews in the ancient world. Tacitus says that they nurtured a hatred against all non-Jews, which one would normally reserve only for one's enemies; and the Egyptian Apion, a contemporary of Paul, is quoted by the Jewish historian Josephus as saying that the Jews swear by their Creator to show no good will toward the Gentiles.[2]

Though in external form both Paul's and such Gentiles' statements against the Jews are similar, the specific context of Paul's words should caution us against viewing them as an indiscriminate anti-Jewish polemic and using them as grounds for collective prejudice and discrimination. For just as the Gospel of John uses the term "the Jews" to designate the Pharisaic-Sadducean leadership which opposed Jesus, rather than Judaism as a whole, so Paul has in mind those Jews who opposed his mission (2:16). Thus we see that Paul's denunciation of "the Jews" takes place within a specific historical context, and it should in no way be generalized. Only when such statements are used indiscriminately in the service of generalized prejudice—as they often have been in the past—can they be called anti-Semitic.

Notes

[1] *Webster's New World Dictionary* (New York: The World Publishing Co., 1967).

[2] Cited by F. F. Bruce, *1 & 2 Thessalonians*, Word Biblical Commentary 45 (Waco, Tex.: Word, 1987), p. 47.

CHAPTER 42

The Man of Lawlessness

*Don't let anyone deceive you
in any way, for that day will not come
until the rebellion occurs and the man
of lawlessness is revealed, the man
doomed to destruction.*
2 THESSALONIANS 2:3

Who is *"the man of lawlessness"?* *Paul does not tell us. So the* problem for the present-day reader is one of identification. Who is this figure whom Paul apparently expects his readers in the church at Thessalonica to recognize?

We must remember what we said in the introduction that Paul's letters are "occasional" documents, sometimes written in response to issues or questions brought to Paul by his churches. They are thus "fragments" of a "conversation." And since we are not privy to that larger conversation, we do not have the same body of information at our disposal which helped the Thessalonian Christians to "decode" Paul's terms. To them Paul could write: "when I was with you I used to tell you these things" (2:5). That was enough to refresh their memory. For us, the meaning of Paul's terms must be discerned, if possible, by giving attention to (1) the issue he addresses and (2) the beliefs of both Judaism and early Christianity behind that issue.

Both of Paul's letters to the Thessalonians are in response to questions about the return of Christ. In the first few decades the faith of these earliest Christians was energized by the lively hope and expectation of the imminent return of the Lord. The new era, announced by Israel's prophets and inspired seers, had dawned in Jesus' life and ministry (1 Cor 10:11). His resurrection was a sign that the power of death was defeated (Acts 2:24), and that these "last days" (Acts 2:17), inaugurated by his life, death and resurrection, would soon come to their culmination (1 Cor 7:29) in the glorious Second Coming of Christ (Acts 3:20). Paul shared with others the belief that this culmination might happen within their lifetime (1 Thess 4:15).

In light of these convictions, certain experiences and events raised troubling questions for the Christians in Thessalonica. From what Paul says in 1 Thessalonians 4:13-14, we can assume that members of their fellowship had died. Would they be excluded from the glorious event of Christ's Second Advent? Paul's answer to that concern is that at Christ's coming those who belong to him, even though they have died ("the dead in Christ"), will be raised from the dead and gathered in one fellowship with those who are still living and will meet the returning, exalted Lord (1 Thess 4:16-17).

In the second letter we hear about fears stirred up among believers by some voices within the church who claimed that the "day of the Lord" had already come (2:2). Such a claim was unsettling and alarming, for it implied that they had been excluded from the event of Christ's return and "shut out from the presence of the Lord and from the majesty of his power" (1:9). Paul calls that claim "deceitful" (2:3), asserting that certain events which precede Christ's coming have yet to occur.

In describing these events (2:3-10) Paul first mentions "the man of lawlessness." He is apparently the key figure in a general rebellion (2:3) who exalts himself both above the so-called gods of heathen worship and "sets himself up in God's temple, proclaiming himself to be God" (2:4). His coming "will be in accordance with the work of Satan" and accompanied by "all kinds of counterfeit miracles, signs and wonders" (2:9), as well as "every sort of evil" (2:10). He is "doomed to destruction" (2:3) at the hands of the Lord Jesus (2:8).

This depiction of "the lawless one" within the context of a rebellion against God has affinities with related concepts in Judaism and early Christianity. The "lawless one" is anticipated in the vision of Daniel 11, where a future ruler is said to exalt himself above all gods (11:36-37) and to desecrate the temple (11:3). Jewish Christians would also have remembered that the celebrated Maccabaean revolt against the Syrian overlords in 167-164 B.C. was provoked by the Syrian monarch Antiochus IV, who claimed that he was "God manifest" and defiled the temple. Other adversaries of Israel and its God had earlier been depicted as exalting themselves and seeking divine status (see Ezek 28:2 and Is 14:13-14).

About a decade before Paul wrote to Thessalonica, the emperor Caligula had attempted to erect a statue of himself in the Jerusalem temple. His claim to divine honor, underscored by this attempt showed the absolute rejection of God concentrated in an individual and provided a foreshadowing of what could be expected from "the man of lawlessness" in the future.

The more immediate parallel to this figure in early Christian thought is that of the Antichrist in John's epistles, a figure associated with the culmination of history ("the last hour"), who denies both God and Christ (1 Jn 2:18-22). Like the lawless one in Paul's letter, the Antichrist is a deceiver (2 John 7). And just as "lawlessness" is at work already prior to the historical revealing of "the man of lawlessness," so the "spirit of antichrist" is already at work prior to the personal, incarnate form of that spirit (1 Jn 4:3).

Paul's word that the coming of the lawless one "will be in accordance with the work of Satan" (2:9) is paralleled by an assertion in the intertestamental apocalyptic work the Martyrdom of Isaiah. In this work, Beliar, the "ruler of this world," is called "the angel of lawlessness" (2:4).

In light of this religious and historical background, Paul's words about the appearing of "the man of lawlessness" prior to the second advent of Christ express the belief that demonic opposition to God, already present in the world, though in a restrained way, will ultimately reach a peak and become incarnated in a historical person who will lead a massive anti-Christ movement.

For Paul and his Thessalonian disciples, the appearing of this figure lay in the future. For Christians in subsequent decades who endured persecution at the hands of Rome and its emperors, the spirit of antichrist, if not the Antichrist himself, was seen as personified in the persecuting Caesars. Frequently, throughout subsequent church history, both secular and religious leaders have been identified as this "man of lawlessness" or "antichrist."[1]

These attempts to discover the lawless one along the stream of history have clearly not been successful, revealing that such undertakings are likely presumptuous and futile. When he is *revealed*, believers will recognize this final incarnation of evil. In the meantime, they are called to be present in the world in such a way that the spirit of lawlessness is resisted and the strongholds of evil's dominion challenged.

Note

[1]See the concise study of the figure of Antichrist in the New Testament and subsequent Christian history by F. F. Bruce, *1 & 2 Thessalonians*, Word Biblical Commentary 45 (Waco, Tex.: Word, 1982), pp. 179-88.

CHAPTER 43

The One Who Holds Back Lawlessness

For the secret power of lawlessness
is already at work;
but the one who now holds it back
will continue to do so till
he is taken out of the way.
2 THESSALONIANS 2:7

The figure of "one who holds back lawlessness" appears in a text where Paul speaks about events and experiences which precede and accompany the Second Coming of Christ (2 Thess 2:1-12). One event is the appearance of "the man of lawlessness" (2:3), a final personal incarnation of evil who will be overthrown "by the breath" of the Lord Jesus at his coming (2:8). That event is still to come, contends Paul. Yet, the reality and power of lawlessness is already present, though not as obviously as it will be when it reaches its climax in "the man of lawlessness."

The previous chapter should be read as background for this one.

The context of this passage shows that "lawlessness" is to be understood as opposition to God, as everything which violates the purposes of God for the creation. "Lawlessness" is at work wherever human beings "refuse to love the truth" (2:10) and "delight in wickedness" (2:12).

This lawlessness is a present reality, but it is being restrained, held in check by a figure whom Paul vaguely refers to as "one who now holds it back." Who is this?

As pointed out in chapter 42 with respect to "the man of lawlessness," so with this enigmatic "restrainer," Paul assumes that the Thessalonian believers are aware of whom he speaks. "During my visit with you," he reminds them, "I used to tell you these things" (2:5). But since we were not there, Paul's veiled reference leaves us groping for that figure's identity. In that task we are not alone. As early as the fifth century, the church father Augustine admitted that the meaning of our "hard saying" completely escaped him, and as eminent an exegete as F. F. Bruce is sure with Augustine that the best we can do is "guess at its meaning."[1] Such guessing, however, is not totally subjective, for we have enough of Paul's view of things from his extensive writings to provide at least some clues.

In the history of this text's interpretation, two interpretations of the "restrainer of lawlessness" have commended themselves as most probable. One view sees in this enigmatic figure a reference to the power of the Roman Empire, represented in the person of the emperor. The state exists, Paul held, for the purpose of restraining wickedness (Rom 13:1-5). In the execution of this purpose the state is an instrument in the hands of God. When it violates that mandate, promoting evil and suppressing the good, it is demonic and the instrument of Satan (see Rev 13).

At the time of his missionary work in Macedonia, not long before he wrote his epistles to Thessalonica, Paul had experienced the protecting benefits of Roman citizenship (Acts 16:35-

39). Later the progress of the gospel in Corinth was shielded from the power of lawlessness by a Roman magistrate (Acts 18:12-17), and Paul's life was saved from certain death at the hands of an angry mob and for several more years of missionary work by Roman authorities in Palestine (Acts 22—23). These experiences of the apostle no doubt confirmed the conviction that, within the sovereign purposes of God, the Roman state, with its laws and extensive power, acted as a restraint against a full manifestation of the powers of lawlessness and evil. He knew that this restraining power would not last forever. Caesar would one day be "taken out of the way" (2:7). But that day was not yet (2:3, 8).

A second interpretation of the "restraining power" (2:6) and the "restrainer" (2:7) takes its clues from another very important dimension of Paul's teaching. In the epistle to the Christians in Rome—written several years after the Thessalonian correspondence and from the same city, Corinth—Paul shares his belief that the proclamation of the gospel to the Gentiles was God's plan and that its rejection by the Jews was temporary (Rom 11:13-32). That belief is in keeping with Jesus' word that the gospel would be preached to all nations before the end would come (Mt 24:14; Mk 13:10). Within this understanding, the proclamation of the good news and its operation in the lives of believers would act as a restraint against evil in the world. Paul, as the apostle to the Gentiles, would be "the one who holds evil back" by his evangelistic ministry.

Both of these interpretations are possible within Paul's overall thought. Two considerations make the latter one somewhat less probable. First, since Paul speaks quite clearly about his gentile mission and purposes elsewhere, the somewhat oblique reference to the something and someone who holds back evil in the present is difficult to understand. On the other hand, his reticence to name this reality explicitly, if Paul has Rome in mind, makes sense. For to say openly that Rome would be "taken out of the way" could cause unnecessary difficulty. Second, it is clear that the one who removes the restraining reality is God. But would Paul speak about his missionary work and the proclamation of the gospel—which he saw as mandated by the Lord—as being taken out of the way by God? It is thus more probable that "the one who holds back lawlessness" is a reference to the state—in the first instance, Rome, but in a larger sense all civil authority which, when properly fulfilling its mandate, acts as a restraint against anarchy.

Note

[1] F. F. Bruce, *1 & 2 Thessalonians*, Word Biblical Commentary 45 (Waco, Tex.: Word, Books, 1982), p. 175.

CHAPTER 44

No Women Teachers

A woman should learn in quietness and full submission. I do not permit a woman to teach or to have authority over a man; she must be silent.

1 TIMOTHY 2:11-12

This is indeed a *"hard saying." The* language *is seemingly straight-*forward and rather clear. But does Paul really mean what we are inclined to think he means? And if he does mean it, is this an instruction which he intended for universal application, regardless of historical context and circumstances?

This passage, and the one discussed in the following chapter, are at the heart of the ongoing discussion of the place and role of women in church, home and society. Answers to the above questions are critical in that discussion.

Chapter 27 on 1 Corinthians 14:33-34 is helpful background for this chapter.

This passage is a difficult one for yet another reason, namely, an emotional/experiential one. As a male, I am sure I cannot fully grasp the impact this apostolic word must have on women. But given that limitation, I can nonetheless understand something of the damage to one's self-worth and sense of giftedness this restrictive word must evoke. We are living at a point in history in which both women and men are recognized as equally gifted in intellectual ability and communication skills. In such a climate, the apostolic prohibition seems particularly difficult to understand and accept. For what is it about gender which militates against the full expression of the Creator's gifts of heart and mind and spirit?

This latter question has often been answered with the assertion that clearly defined roles for men and women are divinely ordained and that Paul's restrictive instruction is evidence of such a universal norm. That response, however, is problematic. The account of the creation of male and female in Genesis 1—2 —which we take as a foundational theological statement of the Creator's design and intention—affirms male and female as equal and complementary. Both are bearers, together, of God's image (1:26-27). Both are given the mandate to responsible sovereignty over the created order (1:28). The creation of the woman is intended to rescue the man from his aloneness and to provide him with a complement (2:18).[1]

Over against an ancient view that the gods played a trick on man by creating woman of inferior material, the creation account of Genesis affirms the woman to be of the same essence as man ("bone of my bone and flesh of my flesh"—Gen 2:23). Thus the view that God intended the woman for a restricted role in home, church and society cannot be grounded in the order of creation.

A restricted status for woman has been traditionally grounded in the account of the Fall (Gen 3) in both Jewish and Christian thought and practice. But it is clear from the context of Genesis

2—3 that the words of 3:16—"Your desire will be for your husband, and he will rule over you"—do not announce God's created design for a male hierarchy. Rather these words announce a cursed existence because of a broken relationship between the human creation and the Creator. A restricted place for woman, and male-over-female dominance, is thus not divine purpose but an expression of human sin.

For Paul, the purpose of Christ's redemptive work was to set God's creation free from the curse of Eden. Those "in Christ" were new creations (2 Cor 5:17), freed from the bondage of sin and its expression in human relationships (Rom 6:5-7). In the new humanity created in Christ, the culturally and religiously ingrained view that some human beings, on the basis of gender or race or social status, were in some sense inferior could no longer be maintained (Gal 3:26-28). That was surely Paul's central theological conviction.

In discussing the passage in 1 Cor 14:33-44, where Paul instructs women in the church to "remain silent," we saw that this restriction was not universally applied either by Paul or by other early congregations. Women functioned in prominent leadership positions (Phoebe, Lydia, Euodia, Syntyche, Priscilla, Junia), designated as ministers (or deacons—Rom 16:1), fellow workers (Rom 16:3), colaborers in the gospel (Phil 4:2-9), apostles (or messengers—Rom 16:7). The Spirit of God empowered both men and women to be proclaimers of God's redemptive work in Christ (Acts 2:14-18). Women's participation in the edifying presentation of the gospel and vocal prayer in the congregation were a normal part of early church life (1 Cor 11).

In light of the above considerations, reasons for the particular restriction imposed on women in Timothy's congregation must be discovered from within the text and the situation in the church which Paul addresses. If, as we have seen, a curtailed role for women was neither a part of the divine intention in creation nor a normative aspect of the redeemed order, then the curtailment of their speaking and teaching and leading—in 1 Corinthians 14 and 1 Timothy 2—must be in response to critical, local situations. Investigation of 1 Corinthians 14 (in chapter 27 above) revealed such a crisis setting in Corinth. A critical situation in the life and faith of Timothy's congregation seems likewise the reason for Paul's instruction here.[2]

Upon reading 1 Timothy, one becomes immediately aware that the integrity of the Christian faith is at stake. There are some in the church who teach false doctrines and are occupied with myths and other speculative ideas which militate against sound and sincere faith (1:3-4). Some have wandered into vain debates, seeking to be teachers without understanding and discernment (1:6-7). There is throughout a concern for maintaining and guarding the truth of the faith (1:19; 2:4-7; 3:14-16; 4:1-3, 6-7, 16; 6:1-5, 12).

We do not know the identity of the false teachers or the full content of their teaching. From the instructions given, we can conclude that the false teaching led to a disregard for proper decorum and practices in the church (2:8-15) as well as to a rejection of the institution of marriage (4:3). In light of this last aspect of the heretical teaching, it is noteworthy that particular attention is directed to young widows (in 5:9-15), who are urged to marry, have children and manage their homes (5:14). When these normal, socially prescribed roles and functions are neglected or rejected, these women are prone to "gossiping" and being "busybodies, saying things they ought not to" (5:13).

On the basis of this data, at least two reconstructions of the situation in Timothy's congregation at Ephesus are possible: (1) It is possible that women in the church at Ephesus were the primary advocates and promoters of the heretical teachings which were upsetting accepted patterns of congregational and home life. (2) A second possibility is that the women in the church had been particularly influenced by the heretical teachers. Such a situation in the Ephesian church is addressed in 2 Timothy 3:6-9 where women, the special targets of those "who oppose the truth," (3:8) become "unable to acknowledge the truth" (3:7).

In either case, Paul's restrictive word in 1 Timothy 2:11-12 must be understood within a context where false teaching is at issue. The general prohibition against all those who "teach false doctrines" (1:3) is now focused specifically on the women who have fallen prey to such false teaching or who are involved in its promulgation.

The admonition of 2:11—"learn in quietness and full submission"—is thus directed at the women who, on the basis of the heretical teaching, have become loud voices, strident advocates of ideas which are upsetting the ordered contexts of congregational and home life. The "submission" enjoined on them is most likely a submission to the elders in the church, who are guardians of the truth and ordered worship. The prohibition against their teaching (2:12) is occasioned by their involvement in false teachings. Finally, the prohibition against "authority over a man" (2:12) must be understood within the context of their rejection of the authority of others, probably the male leaders in Ephesus whose orthodox, authoritative teaching is being undermined by their heretical views. The unusual Greek word used carries primarily the negative sense of "grasping for" or "usurping authority." Thus, the restriction of women's place and participation in the life and ministry of the church at Ephesus is most probably "directed against women involved in false teaching who have abused proper exercise of authority in the church (not denied by Paul elsewhere to women) by usurpation and domination of the male leaders and teachers in the church at Ephesus."[3]

Paul goes on to ground this instruction in reflections on selected passages from Genesis. Those reflections are the subject of our discussion in the next chapter.

Notes

[1]The Hebrew word translated "helper" (in Genesis 2:18 and 2:20), as a designation for the woman, is used only 16 more times in the Hebrew Bible. In those cases, it is always a designation of God as the one who saves, upholds, sustains his people (as in Psalm 46:1). There is no sense in which this word connotes a position of inferiority or subordinate status. The word translated "suitable for" literally means "in front of," signifying one who stands "face to face" with another, qualitatively the same, his essential equal, and therefore his "correspondent."

[2]See Gordon D. Fee, *1 and 2 Timothy, Titus*, Good News Commentary (San Francisco: Harper & Row, 1984), who makes a persuasive case for 1 Timothy as an occasional letter addressing specific heretical teachings.

[3]David M. Scholer, "1 Timothy 2:9-15 and the Place of Women in the Church's Ministry," in Alvera Mickelsen, ed., *Women, Authority & the Bible* (Downers Grove, Ill.: InterVarsity Press, 1986), p. 205. This essay, and several others in this volume, present an excellent study of the exegetical, historical-cultural and linguistic issues in our "hard saying" and related biblical texts.

· C H A P T E R   4 5 ·

Salvation through Childbirth

For Adam was formed first, then Eve.
And Adam was not the one deceived;
it was the woman who was deceived and became a sinner.
But women will be saved through childbearing—
if they continue in faith, love and holiness with propriety.
1 TIMOTHY 2:13-15

When the writer of 2 Peter claims that there are some passages in Paul's writings which "are hard to understand" (3:16), it is easy to imagine that he had 1 Timothy 2:13-15 in mind. The passage has been more intensely debated and analyzed than almost any other single text in the Bible. Its difficulties have caused many interpreters simply to "pass by on the other side." My purpose in this chapter is not to lead the reader through the maze of the discussion and present a smorgasbord of interpretive options.[1] Rather I will rather seek to focus on the central issues and attempt to understand the main point of the passage within the situation Paul is addressing.

Since 2:13 begins with the connective particle "for . . .", it is clear that the following sentences are a continuation of what precedes. Thus this text gives Paul's biblical reflections which provide a rationale for his prohibition against women teaching and usurping authority in the church (2:11-12). We discussed that prohibition in the previous chapter (44).

The conclusion of that discussion was that Paul was addressing problems of heresy in the church at Ephesus and that the women in this congregation were strongly captivated by these false doctrines or were vocal proponents. This teaching led to the questioning and rejection of culturally accepted norms and roles for men and women, causing difficulties for this young congregation within its social context. Paul is concerned that their witness to the truth of the gospel is thereby undermined. He is concerned with "propriety" (2:9, 15), that is, socially acceptable behavior; with the possibility of being "disgraced" in the sight of outsiders (3:7); and with giving "the enemy no opportunity for slander" (5:14; 6:1).

Paul's restrictive admonitions regarding women must be understood within this particular historical situation. They are therefore not to be understood as divine imperatives, applicable universally to all women in all cultural contexts and historical circumstances. Rather, they are authoritative apostolic counsel, given for the correction of abuses in a particular situation which threatened the truth of the gospel and the viability of a young church in an antagonistic environment. The transcendent principle standing behind Paul's particular instructions is the imperative of the gospel (applicable in *all* cultural contexts), namely, God's intention that "all be saved" (2:4; see also 1 Cor 10:33).

Insofar as specific expressions of their new freedom in Christ resulted in the undermining of social conventions (as in rejection of marriage and domestic responsibilities), the undermining of truth (as in teaching of false doctrines) and a domineering pres-

ence (as in usurping authority from the designated leaders of the
church), women were threatening the church's credibility and
therefore its missionary effectiveness. That is the reason Paul
imposes limits.

But why does Paul ground all this in Scripture? Why argue for
priority for the male on the basis of Genesis 2? Why does he
reason from the woman's participation in the Fall (Gen 3) to a
restricted role for her in the church? And finally, what is the
point about women being saved through childbearing?

Answers to those questions begin to emerge when we recognize an essential truth of Paul's life: He was a rabbi who had been
transformed into a follower of Christ. As a trained rabbi he
became a disciple of Jesus and an apostle to the Gentiles. His
training as a rabbi—gained as a student of Gamaliel, one of the
great rabbinic teachers in first-century Palestine (Acts 22:3)—
was placed at the service of the interpretation and articulation of
the gospel. Thus Paul's writings are thoroughly pervaded by
scriptural citations or allusions.

One of the chief functions of the rabbinic tradition was to
respond to the broad range of concerns within the community
of faith, from the most minute aspects of everyday life to the
deepest theological issues. Over hundreds of years of such rabbinic reflection on the biblical text (our Old Testament), a massive body of biblical interpretations accumulated. Some of this
material is reflected in the Jewish intertestamental literature,
including the Apocrypha, a group of writings which was part of
the Greek Old Testament read by the early church. Paul was heir
to that tradition.

At critical points, where the essence and integrity of the gospel
was at stake, Paul uncompromisingly broke with that tradition,
as his Lord had done during his earthly life.[2] But in matters
which were not at the heart of the gospel, or when he gave
instructions for particular situations, he sometimes used inter-

pretations of Old Testament texts which were familiar to him from that tradition.

When we read 1 Timothy 2:13-14, we realize two things immediately. First, Paul does not quote the biblical passages directly. He gives us rather a particular and partial understanding of the meaning of those passages. Second, the situation which he is addressing is a limited, local situation which calls for a limited, partial use of the biblical material. Let us explore these matters in greater detail.

The reason he instructs women to be silent, not to teach and not to usurp authority over men (2:12) is because Adam was formed before Eve (2:13). The Genesis 2 creation narrative is of course referred to here. Within the synagogue, which provided a model for early church life and structure, male dominance was traditionally certified by a reading of the *chronological sequence* of Genesis 2 in terms of male *priority*.

It is clear that Paul does not intend this interpretation of Genesis 2—which he uses here to give authority to his instructions— to be applied universally. For in 1 Corinthians 11, where Paul argues for women's head covering, also on the basis of the chronological sequence in Genesis 2 (11:8-9), he then goes on to admonish his readers that the origin of *both* male and female is in God, and that since the creation every male emerges from, and is therefore preceded by, a female (11:12). In this argument, Paul goes beyond the traditional rabbinic interpretation based on chronological priority, to the heart of the Genesis 2 narrative. For its focus is on the fact that the male, in his chronological priority, is pronounced as "not good" (Gen 2:18). It is the creation of the female as one "corresponding to him" which saves the male from his aloneness.[3]

Thus a traditional interpretation of Genesis 2 is addressed to a specific, limited situation. And it is authoritative primarily for that situation. If, as we have held, women were creating havoc in the congregation by rejecting socially accepted roles and were grasping for authority, especially as those who were peddling heretical teachings, then it was natural for Paul to emphasize biblical texts and interpretations which affirmed culturally and religiously accepted views of female roles.

A further argument for women's restricted place, given in 2:14, is that Eve was deceived and became a sinner, while Adam was not. Here, as in the appeal to Genesis 2 above, Paul refers to a truth expressed in Genesis, this time in the story of the Fall in chapter 3. In Genesis 3:13, Eve says that "the serpent deceived me, and I ate." From this the rabbinic tradition reasoned that women were by nature more vulnerable to deception than men. That view of womanhood was widespread in Judaism. Philo, the important Alexandrian Jewish scholar who was a contemporary of Paul, expressed the view that since woman "is more accustomed to be deceived than man" and "gives way and is taken in by plausible falsehoods which resemble the truth," the proper relation of a wife to a husband is epitomized in the verb "to serve as a slave."[4] In the apocryphal work The Wisdom of Ben Sirach (25:24), the author concludes that "from a woman sin had its beginning and because of her we all die."

Yet, side by side with this emphasis in Jewish tradition was the acknowledgment of Adam's full responsibility. In 2 Esdras 7:118 there is the lament: "O Adam, what have you done. For though it was you who sinned, the fall was not yours alone." Paul also knew this part of the tradition, for in Romans 5:12-14 and 1 Corinthians 15:21-22 he makes Adam, rather than Eve, responsible for the entrance of sin. The basis for this emphasis in the interpretation is of course material from Genesis 3, where Adam is with Eve at the fateful moment (3:6), where God holds him responsible for reaching beyond his limits (3:11), and where he was deceived, just like Eve, into transgressing God's command (3:17).

In light of the above data from both Genesis 3 and other Pauline texts, the phrase in 2:14 "Adam was not deceived" is particularly problematic. For it is clear that *he was in fact deceived,* just like Eve. Some interpreters have concluded that Paul has here simply reverted to the dominant rabbinic interpretation which focuses on the woman's deception, letting man off the hook. But that is pitting Paul the rabbi against Paul the Christian; I do not think this is either legitimate or necessary.

Paul is *always* the rabbi who has been baptized into Christ. And in his fellowship with Christ his rabbinic learning is also baptized. As such, it is placed into the service of his missionary work. And this work of the gospel determines the use he makes of rabbinic interpretations of Old Testament material.

His interpretive method and its application in the particular situation at Ephesus *does not mean* that he shared with his rabbinic tradition the view that women were *inherently* more deceivable. This is confirmed by the fact that Paul uses Eve's deception in 2 Corinthians 11:3-4 as an *illustration* of the possibility that *all* believers in Corinth, both men and women, may be deceived and led away from faith in Christ. Thus we see that Paul uses the Eve tradition variously, depending on the problem being addressed.

Once again, it is apparent that the needs of the situation in Ephesus dictated Paul's use of various aspects of the scriptural tradition which, on the whole, was considered authoritative. Since women in Timothy's congregation seem to have been prominent among those who "have wandered away" from the faith and its appropriate expression in life (1:3-7), or those who "have in fact already turned away to follow Satan" (5:15), or those "who are loaded down with sins and swayed by all kinds of evil desires" (2 Tim 3:6). Paul's partial use of the Genesis material and its application to this particular situation is quite understandable.

A final difficulty of this text is the statement that "women will be saved through childbearing" (2:15).[5] What is the meaning of this statement, and how does it function in the context of the whole passage?

First, if there is one truth which Paul spent his entire ministry driving home to his listeners and readers it is this, that salvation is not gained by the performance of functions and duties nor the exercise of specific roles, but by faith in Jesus Christ. It is therefore impossible to conclude that Paul is speaking about personal salvation. That is, women are not saved by any other means than men.

Second, verse 15 is the conclusion to the entire paragraph. In 2:9-14 the specific instructions to women are restrictive and negative. Verse 15 begins with the word "but" (or, better, "yet"), and what is said is apparently intended as a positive affirmation. The various restrictions imposed on women are now qualified. They are not absolute norms, essential conditions determined by gender. Rather, they are necessary adjustments in light of the historical situation, in which the missionary effectiveness of the young churches was at stake.

In Timothy's situation, heretical teaching undermined the validity of marriage. We are not told why. But on the basis of 1 Corinthians 7, where marriage seems to be rejected by the superspiritualists who despise physical, bodily reality, we can conclude that the heretical teaching viewed marriage, and its specific expression in the bearing of children, as negative, or as unworthy of those who were truly spiritual and members of a new community of "saved" persons. Over against that heretical teaching, Paul may be affirming that the bearing of children, which is a woman's natural procreative, life-giving function, does in fact not keep her from full participation in the community of the saved.

Thus women are and will be saved, even as they perform those domestic and maternal roles expected of women in the social-historical context, but rejected by the heretical teachers. It is possible that the heretical teachers and the women who had been deceived by them saw a rejection of normal domestic and maternal roles as evidence that they were truly saved and spiritual. Such a situation makes Paul's strong and difficult restrictive injunctions to the women in Ephesus absolutely necessary, for the heretical teaching and its consequences represented a comprehensive misunderstanding and denial of the gospel.

Notes

[1]For further information on the literature dealing with 1 Timothy 2:11-15 and related biblical texts, see Alvera Mickelsen, ed., *Women, Authority & the Bible* (Downers Grove, Ill.: InterVarsity Press, 1986).

[2]Examples are (1) Jesus' rejection of rabbinic regulations regarding Sabbath observance—which were based on the fourth commandment (Ex 20:8-11)—by focusing on the heart of God's compassion for broken humanity (Jn 5:2-18; Mk 3:1-6) and (2) Paul's rejection of Jewish Christians' attempt to impose ritual requirements, such as circumcision, on Gentile converts, by affirming that salvation is purely by God's grace and the response of faith (Gal 2:11-16).

[3]See note 1 in chapter 44, where the meanings of the significant Hebrew words in this verse are discussed.

[4]Philo *Questions on Genesis* 1.33 (Loeb Classical Library).

[5]The NIV correctly indicates in a footnote that the Greek text reads: "she will be saved through childbearing." In the previous verse (14), the subject is Eve, the singular, representative of womanhood. That singular subject determines the personal pronoun of verse 15: "but she will be saved . . ." However, the sentence goes on in the plural; "if they continue in faith . . ." It is thus clear that Paul sees Eve as representing all women.

• C H A P T E R 4 6 •

Worse
Than an
Unbeliever

*If anyone does not provide for
his relatives, and especially for his
immediate family, he has denied
the faith and is worse
than an unbeliever.*

1 TIMOTHY 5:8

The point of 1 Timothy 5:8 is rather clear. Failure to care for the needs of particular individuals is tantamount to rejection of one's faith. And a person of faith who acts in such a way as to deny that faith in practice is worse than those who never profess faith in the first place.

What creates difficulties for us is the rigorous tone of this instruction and the finality that seems to be attached to one's failure in following the instruction. A related difficulty—in light of Paul's insistence that salvation is by faith and not by works—is the close connection in our text between a very particular action (or "work") and one's faith, and therefore one's salvation.

A careful look at Paul's argument in its larger context and within his thinking about faith and its fruits should alleviate the difficulties.

Our verse is part of a longer passage (5:3-16) in which Paul is concerned about the place and care of widows in the church. In the ancient world, partially due to patriarchal family and social structures, widows were often among the most weak and vulnerable members of society. It is clear from the Old Testament that God has a special concern for the least, the little ones, the oppressed, the powerless. And that concern includes widows (Deut 10:18; 24:17; Psalm 68:5; Is 1:17). From Luke's account of the ministry of Jesus and the early church (Lk 7:11-15; 18:2-8; 21:1-4; Acts 6:1; 9:39), we see that concern for widows naturally continued in the "new Israel," that the Christian community saw care for widows as a special responsibility, and that groups of widows in the churches were particularly involved in good deeds of charity for others in need.

The larger passage, of which our text is a part, reveals this abiding concern for widows. It also shows that particular circumstances called for greater clarity regarding the church's responsibility in this area. Paul distinguishes between "widows who are really in need" (5:3) and those who have family able to care for them (5:4). Given the fact that the early churches, on the whole, were constituted of people who were from the lower socio-economic strata (see 1 Cor 1:26-28), its economic resources cannot have been extensive. Thus the need arose to channel its limited resources to meet the most urgent situations of deprivation. It may even be that the church's compassion for widows was expressed so consistently that charity became something to be expected, even when there was no real need.

In any case, Paul's instruction is that the primary responsibility for the care of widows rests on members of the immediate family (children or grandchildren—5:4). Only when that assistance is not available, when the widow is "left all alone" (5:5), does the larger community become responsible.

Paul grounds that instruction in two ways. Such action is, first of all, "pleasing to God" (5:4). The imperative to care for parents was derived in Judaism from the fifth commandment ("Honor your father and your mother . . ."—Ex 20:12), and obedience to the commandment was understood to bring with it God's blessing. Second, Paul grounds his instruction in a truth stated over and over in the Word of God; namely, that one's faith, one's beliefs, must find expression in concrete action and relationships. Thus, following a harsh rebuke against the emptiness and shallowness of their worship (Is 1:10-16), Isaiah calls on the people to "Seek justice, encourage the oppressed. Defend the cause of the fatherless, plead the case for the widow" (Is 1:17). A right relationship with God is expressed in the doing of justice, the loving of kindness (Mic 6:6) and the demonstration of steadfast love (Hos 6:6). The truest expression of the worship of God is when God's people are involved in letting "justice roll on like a river, righteousness like a never-failing stream!" (Amos 5:24).

This central Old Testament conviction is also at the heart of the message of Jesus and his followers. We shall be known by the fruit we bear (Mt 7:16, 20) and thus bring glory to God (Jn 15:8). The world will know that we are Jesus' disciples if we genuinely love one another (Jn 13:35). If God's forgiving, reconciling work does not find expression in our relationships, then our worship of God is empty (Mt 5:23-24). The fruit of the Spirit in us, says Paul, expresses itself in kindness and the practice of goodness (Gal 5:22). New life in Christ (Col 3:1-3) is to express itself in a life clothed with compassion and kindness (Col 3:12). Faith that is not evidenced in deeds is judged to be dead, inauthentic faith (Jas 2:14-17). Religion which is "pure and faultless is this: to look after orphans and widows in their distress" (Jas 1:27).

Within this larger New Testament perspective, Paul's directive for the care of widowed mothers or grandmothers by children or grandchildren must be understood. They should "learn first of all to put their religion into practice by caring for their own family" (1 Tim 5:4). The reality of our relationship with God most naturally flows over into our human relationships. And the members of our immediate families are the first ones to feel the impact of our relationship with God. The expression "Charity begins at home" is rooted in the conviction that if love of neighbor does not express itself concretely in our closest relationships, then our claim to love God ("our religion") is a lie (1 Jn 4:19-21).

This is why Paul judges a person who does not provide for family members to have "denied the faith" and to be "worse than an unbeliever" (1 Tim 5:8). Though this judgment seems harsh in relation to this particular failure in practical Christian behavior, Paul's concern throughout the letter that Christian life be above reproach from outsiders (2:2; 3:1-7; 5:14; 6:1) helps us to understand his strong word. The phrase "to be worse than an unbeliever" implies that even unbelievers normally are expected to care for those of their own households. Believers who neglect this responsibility are thus acting "worse than" unbelievers. Whenever that happens (see also 1 Cor 5:1-2), the church is not being God's alternative community in a broken, fragmented world. And such a life in the world represents a denial of the faith.

CHAPTER 47

Wine for the Stomach

Stop drinking only water,
and use a little wine
because of your stomach
and your frequent illnesses.
1 TIMOTHY 5:23

In the context of a society in which the abuse of alcohol is such a serious problem, this item in Paul's list of personal advice to Timothy raises for many the question of the legitimacy of the use of alcohol. Since alcohol is so easily abused, and since its abuse leads to the enslavement of people to addiction, should not Christians be encouraged to abstain from any use of it? This latter, prohibitionist view is expressed in a somewhat humorous anecdote from a discussion of this issue among a group of deacons. To the factual affirmation by one deacon that Jesus had turned water into wine at the wedding at Cana (Jn 2), another deacon replied: "Yes, he did, but he shouldn't have!" When the basic premise is the conviction that any use of alcohol is wrong, then Jesus' action and Paul's admonition become problematic.

Paul's word must be understood in the context of other advice in the correspondence with Timothy and Titus. It also must be seen as a sound piece of advice in the cultural context and as an expression of a central biblical principle for Christian living.

Earlier in 1 Timothy, Paul had listed among the characteristics of those who would be leaders in the church that they be "not given to drunkenness" (3:3) or "not indulging in much wine" (3:8). In advice to Titus, elders need to be examples who are "not given to drunkenness" (Tit 1:7), and the elder women in the church are to be taught not to be "addicted to much wine" (literally, "slaves to wine"—Tit 2:3). In all these injunctions, the emphasis is clearly on moderation; namely, a responsible use of alcohol which does not lead to its control of one's life.[1] This is in keeping with a central principle of Christian life stated by Paul in Ephesians 5:18—"Do not get drunk on wine, which leads to debauchery, but be filled with the Spirit." The only legitimate controlling reality in the believer's life is to be God's Spirit. All other controlling realities are, in fact, idolatrous.

In light of these prohibitions against the excessive use of alcohol, Paul's advice to Timothy—"Stop drinking *only* water and use a *little* wine" (emphasis mine)—implies that Timothy may have concluded, from the warnings against excessive use, that total abstinence was called for. It may even be that the false teachers, in their prohibition against certain foods (4:3), had argued for total abstinence.[2]

In any case, Timothy's total rejection of alcohol seems to have had harmful consequences for his health. So Paul, in keeping with his warnings against abusive use, counsels for the use of "a little wine." In this, he is simply reflecting the common use of wine, especially for medicinal purposes, in the ancient world. Its beneficial effects "against dyspeptic complaints, as a tonic, and as counteracting the effects of impure water, were widely recognized in antiquity,"[3] and are confirmed by modern medicine. Paul's view on this matter may have been backed by the advice of his fellow worker Luke, the beloved physician.

Notes

[1]Gordon Fee understands these warnings as "negative reflections on first-century culture itself, which often admired heavy drinkers" (1 and 2 Timothy, Titus, p. 140).

[2]Whether these teachings were grounded in Jewish regulations regarding clean and unclean foods, we do not know. But in the advocacy of an ascetic style of life, the Stoic philosopher Epictetus (A.D. 55-135) taught that one should "drink water only." (Cited by A. J. Hultgren, 1 Timothy, 2 Timothy, Titus, 2 Thessalonians, Augsburg Commentary on the New Testament [Minneapolis: Augsburg, 1984], p. 93.)

[3]J. N. D. Kelly, A Commentary on the Pastoral Epistles (New York: Harper, 1964), p. 129, cites several Jewish and Hellenistic sources, including Hippocrates, who recommended moderate amounts of wine for a patient for whose stomach water alone is dangerous.

CHAPTER 48

Cretans
Are Always
Liars

*Even one of their own prophets
has said, "Cretans are always liars,
evil brutes, lazy gluttons."
This testimony is true.*
TITUS 1:12-13

These sentences strike us at best as extreme, at worst as untrue. The people thus categorized are inhabitants of the island of Crete in the eastern Mediterranean, where Titus is a leader among the churches. Presumably most members of these churches, and especially the elders in those churches, whom Paul expects to be blameless, self-controlled, upright, holy and disciplined (1:8), would not qualify as "liars, evil brutes, lazy gluttons." Even among the general Cretan population there were surely many who led good and upright lives. Thus the definition of Cretans as "always liars" is hardly justified. Though Paul is clearly citing from "one of their own prophets," he supports the generalization by concluding that "this testimony is true." How are we to understand this harsh language? A closer look at the situation addressed in the Cretan churches, as well as the citation's origin and history, should ameliorate, if not eliminate, the difficulty.

The situation addressed is one in which heretical teachers are abroad in the churches, opposing "the knowledge of the truth" (1:1), the promises of God "who does not lie" (1:2), "the trustworthy message" and "sound doctrine" (1:9). They are "deceivers" (1:10), "teaching things they ought not to teach" (1:11), rejecting "the truth" (1:14).

It is this focus on the untruthfulness of the opponents of the gospel and the untruthfulness of their teaching which brings to Paul's mind a line from a revered Cretan, Epimenides, a religious teacher and wonderworker from c. 600 B.C. Paul's designation of him as a "prophet" is probably based on the description of Epimenides as an inspired, prophetic man by Plato, Aristotle and other ancient writers. The ground for Epimenides' unsavory characterization of his fellow Cretans was apparently their popular claim that the tomb of Zeus, the head of the Greek pantheon of gods, was located on their island. This claim was considered false, since Zeus, as a god, could not be dead. By Paul's time, Epimenides' words had become a popular slogan, expressing the widespread reputation of Cretans as untruthful. The verb "to Cretize" became slang for lying or cheating, just as the city of Corinth's reputation for sexual immorality led to the slang verb "to Corinthianize."

As we have seen, the context in which Paul appeals to Epimenides' words is one of crisis. In such a situation of polemical confrontation, exaggerations are common. Paul is obviously angry at the enemies of the truth in the Cretan churches, and he responds to their deceptions by using the typical device of overstatement. What Paul intends to communicate forcefully is clear; namely, in the case of these teachers who peddle false teaching,

Epimenides' dictum is in fact shown to be true.

That Paul's words are not to be understood in an absolute sense (that is, that *every* Cretan is a liar!) is confirmed by the fact that his appeal to Epimenides would otherwise involve a contradiction. For since Epimenides is a Cretan, his statement that "Cretans are always liars" would include him. And that would lead to the conclusion that he *always* lies and that his statement is therefore false. It is clear then that neither Paul nor Epimenides intended the statement to be understood in an all-inclusive general sense.

Scripture Index